Guy Stuff

or

It's OK to Ask for Directions

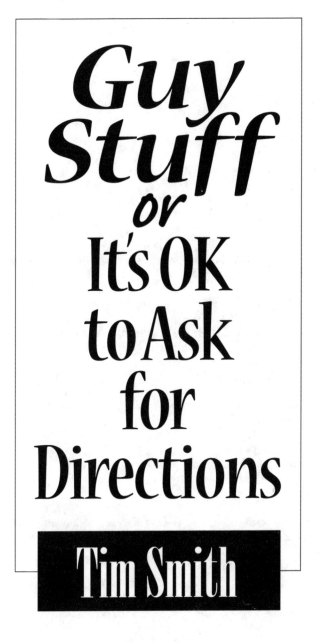

Guy Stuff
or
It's OK to Ask for Directions

Tim Smith

MOODY PRESS
CHICAGO

All Scripture quotations, unless indicated, are taken from the *Holy Bible: New International Version®*. NIV®. Copyright © 1973, 1978, 1984 by International Bible Society. Used by permission of Zondervan Publishing House. All rights reserved.

The "NIV" and "New International Version" trademarks are registered in the United States Patent and Trademark Office by International Bible Society. Use of either trademark requires permission of International Bible Society.

Scripture quotations marked (NLT) are taken from the *Holy Bible, New Living Translation*, copyright © 1996. Used by permission of Tyndale House Publishers, Inc., Wheaton, Illinois 60189. All rights reserved.

Scripture quotations marked (NASB) are taken from the *New American Standard Bible*, © 1960, 1962, 1963. 1968, 1971, 1972, 1973, 1975, 1977 and 1994 by The Lockman Foundaiton, La Habra, Calif. Used by permission.

ISBN: 0-8024-3382-0

1 3 5 7 9 10 8 6 4 2

Printed in the United States of America

To my father, Phil Smith,
who has provided a lifelong example
of a mature Christian man—
one who is tough and tender.

Contents

Guidelines for Real Guys

*G*uys who find fulfillment and purpose in life recognize and follow principles of healthy living, all found in God's Word. The fifteen principles discussed in this book (one per chapter) form guidelines for living as whole men. The principles for becoming real guys are:

1. A real guy—a godly guy—aligns his desires with God's desires.
2. A real guy can be authentic because his confidence is in the Lord, not in his natural strengths.
3. A real guy is consistent inside and out, a mark of his integrity.
4. A real guy has learned to be tough and tender.
5. A real guy demonstrates love by accepting differences in a relationship and acting to meet the needs of the other person.
6. A real guy recognizes that his emotions are a God-given resource for understanding himself and connecting in relationships.
7. A real guy competes fairly and displays self-control, because he has learned to submit to authority.
8. A real guy knows he needs close relationships with other guys if he is to grow as a man.
9. A real guy is humble, for he knows humility will keep him from doing foolish things.
10. A real guy lets God's Spirit empower him with power and love. Through God's Spirit, he develops the self-discipline to balance power with love.
11. A real guy believes that true success is discovering what God is doing and joining God there.
12. A real guy understands that relationships require work. He chooses to work on his two most important relationships: with God and with his wife.
13. As a parent, a real guy meets the needs of his children.
14. A real guy is blameless because he has developed a sense of balance.
15. A real guy will submit humbly to God's process of growing through serving.

Acknowledgments

*M*any friends have helped to shape my understanding of men and their issues. Without their assistance, I wouldn't have much to write about.

Bob Olthoff has been an iron-sharpens-iron friend, along with establishing a solid ministry to men as Pastor to Caring at Calvary Community Church. Gordon Dalbey's books and friendship have been very helpful and inspirational.

My breakfast buddies for years, especially Dan Morgan and Don Cole, have been faithful to ask the difficult questions. In addition, I write, speak, and counsel with conviction knowing that my Prayer Support Team is holding me up before our Father.

Gary Chapman and Norm Wright, authors and gifted counselors, have encouraged me with written and spoken words.

My thanks also to those at Moody Press who helped shaped my ideas and writing. Jim Bell, editorial director, has shown confidence in this project and me. My editor, Jim Vincent, has done another masterful job of making me sound better than I am.

Introduction
Talkin' Guy to Guy

I'm glad you picked up this book. Pretend like it is really interesting; especially if you are browsing in a bookstore. Raise your eyebrows. Smile. Turn the page. *Laugh.* Thanks.

Can we talk, guy to guy?

They asked me to write a "men's book." It sounded like a contradiction to me. Most of us men buy books, but we never read them. OK, I'll be honest: Most of our *wives* buy books for us, and we never read them. So why should I write a men's book? Besides, I'm not a genuine member of The Men's Movement. In fact, I'm wary of anything with the word *movement* in it. In some ways, I don't even consider myself a man yet. Oh sure, I am mature, or at least I am forty-something. Does mileage make you mature?

So this isn't a men's book; don't panic. It's a guy's book; and it's not really a "book" in a literary sense, it's *stuff.* That is why I call it *Guy Stuff.*

If you are still browsing in a public setting, laugh loudly.

Don't worry, I promise not to get too serious or too weird. No bare-chested, bang-the-drum-in-the-forest nonsense (part of that Men's Movement shenanigans). This is guy stuff.

ABOUT OUR STUFF

As guys, we have stuff. We like our stuff. We work hard for the stuff. At the end of a hard day at work, we like nothing more than to come home, have a tasty meal, and play with our stuff.

Guys are defined by their stuff. Their stuff makes up their world. You can tell a lot about a guy by looking in his garage. It's a pastime of mine. I like to drive around neighborhoods and see what people have in their garages. It's not that I'm a vehicular voyeur. I don't care about the cars; I'm interested in the stuff. I like to guess what a guy is about by checking out his stuff. My neighbor, Duane, has the ultimate guy garage. It's a double-deep drive-through. You know, the kind that has *two* garage doors, one at each end. Duane can back his boat in the front garage door and out the back so he can work on it on the car patio in the back. I don't even have a car patio.

You can tell a lot about a guy by looking in his garage. Duane is a cool car guy. His garage has a huge workbench, built-in cabinets, the standard pegboard tool storage system, and enough fluorescent lamps to give him a savage tan in fourteen minutes. It also has every power tool made by Craftsmen and Makita, a complete home gym, and car covers (to keep the dust off while the two cars are *inside* the garage). Did I mention Duane is single?

I am still trying to figure out a guy down the street. All he has in his garage are two cars. He must be some kind of a nut.

All this stuff is nice, but it doesn't help us know who we are. (And as we will see in chapter 1, having a lot of stuff shouldn't define who we are.) Knowing who we are as guys can be challenging. Our culture has done a lot to confuse us. For instance, when have you heard our contemporary media speak favorably of these two words: *Christian man?* It's almost like it's an oxymoron (two

words that don't seem to belong together); can you be a
Christian and a man? Can you be a *man* and a Christian?

BEING A GUY VS. BEING A MAN

Male bashing must be in season. It's trendy to put
down men. In some circles, it's in vogue to make fun of
Christians. Being a Christian man might not be the polit-
ically correct identity. But I'm not going to worry about
that; because this isn't a political book. And it is not a
book about being a *man*. It is a book about being a guy. I
can be a guy. I am a guy. I am a Christian guy. I don't
want the burden of being a *man*—there seems to be too
much baggage with that word.

So let's relax, and not get uptight about becoming more
manlike. Let's just deal with some stuff—some guy stuff.

I went to a men's conference and they talked a lot
about "becoming a *man* of integrity." I liked the idea, but
it scared me. Was I a *man?* I hope to become a *man* of integrity someday, but in the meantime I'm working on becoming a guy of integrity. It seems more realistic. I know
what it means to be a guy. I don't struggle with being a
guy. It's a little fuzzy when we talk about being a *man*.
That word is loaded and means many different things to
different people. Most of us male types are comfortable
being referred to as one of the guys; so let's start there,
learning to be comfortable with who we are now, and
moving toward being a complete guy, someone who actually is a whole man.

How do we do that? How do we become guys of integrity? That is what this book is about.

But first, a caution: please don't worry. I promise not
to be in your face, just on your side. The last thing we
need as guys is more shame. In fact, that is why I wrote
this book—to be encouraging. I hereby declare this book
to be a guilt-free zone. We will take a look at what keeps
us from being all that we can be, and what we can do
about it.

Some of the subjects we'll talk about are: our identity as guys; how to be real in a fake world; how to develop integrity in a cheesy culture; how to perfectly understand women (OK, maybe I was exaggerating on that one); how to know if we are a success; and becoming a spiritual leader.

We'll begin the book with a fairly basic question: Who are you?

1

"You Are What You Do"

$\mathcal{M}$any companies are downsizing, growing smaller, leaner (and sometimes meaner). If you were "downsized' from your job—that is, eliminated—would your identity be downsized? Without a job, would your identity change? It would if your identity depended on your job.

Some guys are nervous because they don't know who they are apart from their job. Their sense of identity, purpose, and contribution are vitally connected to their work. They believe, or their friends believe, "You are what you do."

A lot of guys struggle with their identity. To a guy, what he does often determines who he is: a fireman, an accountant, a sales rep, or a software engineer. Most guys base their identities on their jobs or their abilities. Who they are is what they do. If they perform well, they feel good about themselves. If they produce, they like who they are.

Most guys need to work; it's the way we are made. But it doesn't have to define who we are. It certainly won't give us a lasting identity or meaning. I have met men who were successful in their careers and have acquired wealth but were still needy. They still were searching for their identity. They were asking, "Who am I?"

Counselor H. Norman Wright says that when men struggle with identity, asking, "Who am I?" they are asking the wrong question:

The right question is, "Where am I?" because that question points to our identity in relation to God Himself. Patrick Morley has said: "We are who we are because of where we are." Many men hearing this take their task-oriented male perspectives and begin asking, "Then what can I start doing for God?" Again, the wrong question. It is not doing things for God. It is simply being with Him. If a man is task-oriented in his relationship with God, he will be asking, "What is the purpose of my life?" A more important question is, "*Who* is the purpose for my life?" That question focuses on a man's relationship with Jesus Christ. By answering the second question first, the first question is easier to answer.[1]

Have you ever asked yourself, "Who is the purpose for my life?" For many of us guys, we would say, "I am the purpose of my life." We exist primarily for ourselves. To think of living for another person is foreign to many of us. It goes against our cultural messages that tell us what a man is: "A man is a rugged individual"; "A real man doesn't need anyone—except maybe his horse."

LIVING FOR SOMEONE ELSE

To live for someone else seems strange but that is what being a Christian is all about: "I myself no longer live, but Christ lives in me. So I live my life in this earthly body by trusting in the Son of God, who loved me and gave himself for me" (Galatians 2:20 NLT).

Read those first five words again, "I myself no longer live." Haunting. Penetrating. Abrupt.

If we are to discover who we are in Christ, we must first be willing to have a funeral for our former selves. Our old identities, which were task-oriented, performance-based, and job-dependent, need to be put to death.

For many years, I asked myself, "Who am I?" I wanted to know my identity. I was looking for clues from others to define myself. "I am not like that guy." "I am better than that loser." "I am not as rich as him." "He doesn't have the education I have." "He seems to have his act totally together." It's depressing playing the Comparison Game; you always wind up the loser.

If we keep asking the "Who am I?" question, it doesn't satisfy. It doesn't work because it's the wrong question. We need to ask, "Where am I with God?" This is a much better question, because not only does it address the search for our identity, but it also deals with our quest for purpose. "Where am I with God?" is the question because it addresses our identity and why we are here. Many men struggle with "Why am I here?" That is a purpose question. You could spend twenty years of your life searching for your identity and twenty more years looking for your purpose. Or you could ask yourself, "Where am I with God?" and deal with the two critical issues at once.

God created Adam because He wanted a relationship. God is a relationship-seeking God. God didn't create Adam because He needed someone to take care of His garden. With God, relationship comes first, work comes second. When we focus on our relationship with God as our number one priority, other issues, including our identity and purpose, take their proper role. If we mess up with the number one priority, all the fuss and quest for identity and purpose will be wasted effort.

I have seen many guys waste time trying to impress others because they weren't sure about themselves; they hadn't dealt with the number one priority, "Where am I with God?" As businessman Patrick Morley observes, "Today men are consumed by desires to buy things they don't need, with money they don't have, to impress people they don't like."[2]

It rings true, doesn't it? We work hard to project certain images of ourselves. I believe we get caught up in the performance trap because we haven't come to terms with our identity in relationship with God. At church, we might project the confident and smiling Christian buddy persona. At work, we might play the role of the capable and dedicated employee. At home, we maintain our image of the devoted and loving family man. We could have three or more roles to play in our life. No wonder we find ourselves in an identity crisis! If these roles are not true to our genuine self, they can be very exhausting. Acting is very fatiguing. Projecting different images to different people can be very demanding of our emotional and mental resources.

Morley, author of *The Man in the Mirror*, calls these varying roles "the visible you," and he believes the visible you masks the real you, which is known only to God:

> The visible you is the known you. It is never the real you. We have learned to speak and act in ways that allow us to cope with our world and peacefully coexist. We work hard to project a certain image of ourselves to others. The real you is the you that is known by God. We are who we are in our minds first, before we speak or act. Our speech and actions are the result of our thinking. Scripture tells us, "The heart is deceitful above all things and beyond cure. Who can understand it?" (Jeremiah 17:9) To protect our self-image we kid, trick, and fool ourselves into believing the visible you is somehow real. To see ourselves as we really are, we must acknowledge our inability to do so without God's help.[3]

It's back to that "I myself no longer live" scenario. We are not ourselves until we find ourselves in Christ. Are you willing to discover your true identity? Are you ready to step off the stage and quit the performance? When we are willing to die to ourselves we can be reborn with our identity as God's sons. Stand up straight! You are a child of the King. You are a prince! Now start acting like one.

IN SEARCH OF SIGNIFICANCE

Henry David Thoreau said, "The mass of men live lives of quiet desperation."

You might respond, "That's easy for Thoreau to say.

Wasn't he the guy who lounged beside a pond and thought deep thoughts? I don't have that luxury. I have a wife, two kids, two car payments, and a mortgage. I got to get to work."

Could it be that our busyness leads to our desperation? And could it be quiet desperation because we don't have the time, place, or person to talk with?

That was the case with Howard, one of my friends from church. The father of two fine teenagers in our youth group, he met me at church one day for a lunch appointment.

"Hop in," Howard said as he opened the shiny black door to his BMW.

"Thanks, Howard,." I answered. "Is this new?"

"Yeah, I traded the old one in for this. It had too much mileage; I didn't want to depreciate it too much." Howard was always thinking investment. He had done well at his sales career, and he had all the toys to prove it. Today we were going out to lunch at his request.

"So, where do you want to eat, Tim?"

"Someplace outside. I have been cooped up in my office all morning."

We drove to a harborside cafe. The hostess seated us outside at a table with a terrific view of the passing sailboats and cruisers.

"Will this work?" asked Howard, somewhat sarcastically.

"Perfect. Hey, look at that Catalina. Isn't that like yours?"

"Yeah, mine is a few feet longer."

Howard didn't seem that interested in the passing sailboat. In fact, he seemed a little perturbed.

"What's up?" I ventured.

"I have been doing some heavy thinking."

Occasionally, Howard's sixties vocabulary kicked in.

"About?"

"Life." He smiled at his brevity.

"And?"

"Well . . . I just don't know. I'm not satisfied," he scowled as he sipped his ice tea.

I couldn't believe my ears. Here was a man who had it all: a successful career; the admiration of others; a beautiful wife; and two healthy, athletic teenage kids. Who wouldn't be satisfied with that?

"What brought this on?"

"Frankly, you did."

I was shocked. "What? What do I have to do with it?"

"Well, you took our kids to Mexico for the mission trip, and they loved it. It changed them. They found that they had something to offer. In a word, they found significance. The kids in Mexico responded to my two teenagers. I have never seen them so enthusiastic. What did you do to my kids?"

"I gave them an opportunity to serve. Serving leads to significance. Too many of our kids are never asked to serve. They are served. That's why many feel insignificant."

"Boy, I have seen that a lot in our city. I think that could be why so many kids are on drugs down at the high school."

"I think you are right, Howard. When people don't feel significant, they get desperate."

"It seems like our culture does a good job of helping people pursue individual rights, but not as good of a job with helping us build community and offer service."

"That's what the church can offer. In fact, we have to," I explained. "If we don't provide ministry and mission for these kids, they will live desperate lives, without significance."

"What about me?" pleaded Howard sincerely.

"You want to go to Mexico?" I kidded.

"Well, if that's what it takes," he smiled.

"Are you interested in discovering how you can serve, like your kids did?"

"Yeah, I think that is what is missing. I have a good job, my wife doesn't have to work, we have a nice house, we are healthy; but something is missing. I want what my kids have."

"Significance?"

Howard nodded his head. "That's it. But not the significance you get for working—that's a treadmill. I'm thinking more along the lines of contribution and service."

"You want your life to count. You want to make a lasting impact."

"Exactly! How did you know?" Howard asked curiously.

"Every guy searches for significance. Some look for it in wealth, position, or in athletics. Most believe that success leads to significance, but that is not always true."

"I know that."

"The difference in guys is in how we pursue satisfying our need for significance. As I see it, there are effective ways and ineffective ways to search for significance. The search can draw us toward God, or pull us away from Him."

"The ineffective ways are hoping that success, money, status, or winning at golf will make you significant, right?"

"Exactly!" I responded. "I feel I am living a life of significance, and you have seen me play golf!"

"It's not a pretty sight," joked Howard, who is an excellent golfer. Then he added: "Your life counts because it is invested in others."

"Bingo! That's what you need," I exclaimed. "We need to find you a place to serve."

"That is what is missing. I have been providing for my family and living for myself."

"Significance is only possible when we involve ourselves with the welfare of others."

We discussed some options and assessed his gifts and

abilities. Within weeks he was ministering as a leader in our high school group. After a few weeks, I asked how things were going.

"Tim, I have discovered that helping these kids is an extension of who I am in Christ. I have never felt more needed. I feel significant. I might quit my job and do this full-time!"

THE MYTH OF THE THREE B'S

Our culture feeds us a lot of myths, especially about who guys are. How much does a myth have to be off the truth to be dangerous? Just a little bit. I like to compare it to sailing. If you are only off a few degrees it won't effect your day sail to Catalina Island twenty-six miles off the coast of California. But if you are off the same few degrees, and you try to sail to Hawaii, you will miss the Hawaiian Islands entirely. Myths, over a long period of time, can leave us lost and confused.

We need to avoid at least three myths. I call them the three B's: brains, brawn, and bucks. The first myth our culture tells us about a guy's worth is that to be valuable you must have brains. We admire the Bill Gates and the Steven Spielbergs of our time. They are brilliant and creative.

There is nothing wrong with being intelligent (some of my friends are). But evaluating our worth by our IQ is dangerous. It isn't always that accurate, and sometimes the standard changes. I know guys with Ph.D.'s who can't get a job, and I know some with only a high school diploma who are millionaires. Basing our worth on how smart we are is a faulty approach.

The second myth we often swallow is that to be valuable you must have brawn (or bulging biceps). Our world is infatuated with the pursuit of the perfect body, or the perfect game. Professional athletes are the icons of the age. What guy wants to be some scrawny wimp of a noodle who has a nice personality? We want to be *studs*.

The problem with this myth is that we all can't be Michael Jordan or Tiger Woods; most of us are destined to be average.

The third myth that we often chase in our pursuit for self-worth is to be valuable you must have bucks. Wasn't it Billy Joel who said, "All you need are looks and a whole lotta money"? Or, as the great philosopher and sage Jerry McGuire exclaimed, "Show me the money!" As guys, we spend most of our days working to bring home the bacon. Our lives are focused on earning and providing. There isn't anything wrong with that; it's when we base our worth on how much we earn that we are in trouble.

Our worth should not be determined by something so fickle as our earnings. Our personal worth should not be defined by our income or the stock market—things always changing and often influenced by dozens of factors beyond our control (or understanding).

Guys are tempted to believe the cultural lies that to be worthwhile, they must have *brains, brawn,* and *bucks.* Contrast these myths with God's penetrating words: "This is what the Lord says: 'Let not the wise man boast of his wisdom or the strong man boast of his strength or the rich man boast of his riches, but let him who boasts boast about this: that he understands and knows me, that I am the Lord, who exercises kindness, justice and righteousness on earth, for in these I delight'" (Jeremiah 9:23–24).

In God's economy, a man has worth when he is wise, when he understands and knows God and what is important to God. A guy becomes a God Guy when he gets excited about what delights God.

Guidelines for Real Guys

Principle 1: A real guy—a godly guy—aligns his desires with God's desires.

2

A Real Man

---

*A*re you lonely? Do you ever feel alone in your ministry?"

I was taken aback by the question. Ron was being very direct. I had only known him for a few months, and I was caught off guard. Should I pretend that I wasn't lonely and deny it (as I had for years)? Besides, how could I be lonely? Thousands of people know me! I ventured forward with honesty.

"Yeah, sometimes I feel lonely. I'm surrounded by people, but it's always in the role as pastor, leader, counselor, or author. I need to be 'just Tim.'"

"Would you like to be in a men's group with me?" asked Ron.

I studied him for a few seconds. He was quite different from me. I wasn't sure I wanted to be in a group with him. He was small, pale, and unathletic. He spent his free time indoors. Why would I want to be in a group with him?

"What kind of group were you thinking about?" I asked, trying to buy more time to decide.

"A small group of about four guys. We could meet weekly for prayer and maybe work through a book. Have you done this before?"

"Yes."

"Was it a positive experience?" Ron asked.

Pleasant memories filled my head. Toast, coffee, and eggs quickly came to mind. I thought of the dozens of guys I used to meet with at Denny's for fellowship and the Grand Slam Breakfast. "Oh, yeah," I heard myself respond, "I used to do it all the time. I guess I got out of the habit. Yes, let's start a group."

It was difficult for me to be real with Ron. It was easier to pretend I wasn't lonely. After all, I was the strong macho man who didn't need anybody. Why should I take the risk of being authentic? What value is there in being real?

Taking the risk to be real is better than the isolation of pretending.

We began meeting weekly; our group grew to four men. We met to stimulate each other "toward love and good deeds," as the Scripture says (Hebrews 10:24). The first book we read was Patrick Morley's *The Man in the Mirror*. We read a chapter each week on our own and discussed it at our group. In this insightful book I discovered why I had been lonely.

> Most men have a friendship "deficit." Their balance sheets are empty when it comes to true friends. Most men don't know how to go about developing a true friend, or how to be one.
>
> We may be surrounded by many acquaintances but lonely for someone to really talk to. We don't have someone to share our deepest dreams and fears with. We don't have anyone who is willing to just listen, to simply be a friend and listen, and not always have a quick solution.
>
> Friends bring risks: rejection, betrayal, embarrassment, hurt feelings. But friends are worth the risk, if we can learn how to find them.[1]

The words leaped out at me: "Most men don't know how to go about developing a true friend, or how to be one." Conviction set in. I was living life without any meaningful relationships with other men. Sure, I had camaraderie with men at work, but I was not in an "iron sharpens iron" situation. If I needed to, I could trick the guys at work. I could bluff my way around the men at church. But I wanted something more than those routine "fine, thank you" and "good to see ya's." I wanted intimacy with other men.

THE CHANT:
"GOOD-TO-SEE-YA-HOW-ARE-YA?"

I remember one of the leaders at a former church. People looked up to him. He was influential. I noticed he had a routine greeting. Every time he saw someone at church he'd chant, "Good-to-see-ya-how-are-ya?" smile and keep on walking. It began to annoy me. I thought that a leader should stop and listen for a response, or otherwise not ask a question in the first place. I was trying to learn authenticity, and this guy seemed fake.

I decided to play around with his routine. The next time I saw him at church, I set my plan in motion.

"Good-to-see-ya-how-are-ya?" He smiled and continued walking.

I smiled back and responded, "Terribly upset, thanks." It didn't even register.

The next time.

"Good-to-see-ya-how-are-ya?" He smiled and continued walking, fast.

This time I snarled (no smile), "FINE—which means Frustrated In No Empathy!"

I had to raise my voice for the last few words because he marched past.

This guy was really bugging me. How he became a leader without much personal concern for people baffled me. Because I am bullheaded, I kept up my experiment. One day he stopped, asked me how I was, and listened with empathy for fifteen minutes. Of course, this is only my imagination. He *never* stopped. He never slowed his pace. I don't think he cared.

I left that church and forgot about him until a friend asked, "Did you hear about Mr. How-are-ya? You know, the leader that annoyed you?"

"No, what about him?"

"Turns out he wasn't such a model citizen and leader after all. He got arrested for embezzling his company."

I was disappointed but not shocked. Perhaps if Mr. How-are-ya had been vulnerable enough to be honest with a Christian brother he could have avoided moral collapse.

GET REAL: FIND A FRIEND
WHO ASKS THE HARD QUESTIONS

The news reinforced for me the need to be accountable to friends who are courageous enough to ask the hard questions and loving enough to listen to the answers.

Do you have that kind of friend? Is there someone you are regularly meeting with who can ask you questions, like:

"Are you living a life of purity?"
"Do you have a heart for Jesus? What are you doing to keep your spiritual life growing?"
"Are you being faithful to your wife?"
"Are you making time for your kids?"
"Are you above reproach and blameless in all your dealings at work?"
"What are you contributing to build God's kingdom?"
"How are you passing on a legacy to your children?"
"How have you recently demonstrated honor to your wife?"

These kinds of questions can be asked only in a small cadre of men who are committed to you and confidentiality. This is risky business. If I am going to be vulnerable with others, I want to be sure I can trust them. "What is said in the group stays in the group" became my group's wise slogan.

Every guy has areas where he continues to struggle as

a man. Each of us needs the help of a Christian brother.
We can't do it alone. To become Christians, we must admit that we don't have it all together—that we need help.
We must admit our need for forgiveness and reconciliation with God. We must be real about our imperfection.

Just as we can't become Christians unless we are real
—honest about our sins and needs—we can't grow as
Christians unless we stay authentic. Similarly, a real man
knows and admits his strengths and weaknesses. A real
man knows he isn't perfect and doesn't try to pretend
that he is. A real man is aware that he needs companionship with other men. As the wise king Solomon wrote:
"Two are better than one, because they have a good return for their work: If one falls down, his friend can help
him up. But pity the man who falls and has no one to
help him up!" (Ecclesiastes 4:9–10).

A friend can help you when you fall. A friend can
keep you from falling. A real man is in an accountable relationship with at least one brother.

HOW TO BE FAKE

We have been sobered by the moral collapse of religious leaders. I have known Christian men who have fall-
en; and most of them were leaders in their churches. As I
researched their demise, I have discovered five common
vices that contribute to moral compromise.

Significantly, these five are common to the inauthen-
tic, or "fake" person. Lots of men choose to be fake
rather than deal with the tensions and challenges of becoming an authentic man. It's easy to be fake. Just en-
gage in the following practices and attitudes, and you
can avoid becoming a real man. You also will miss out on
the joy and fullness of being true to yourself, your God,
and those you know.

First, lack accountability. In our Christian culture we
want to be nice. It's difficult to ask penetrating questions.
We are more comfortable being peacekeepers than truth

tellers. We'd rather convince ourselves that we are "keeping the peace" by being superficial, protective, and
avoiding accountability.

None of the men I knew who had moral failures was
in an accountability relationship. No one in their lives
was asking the tough questions. They isolated themselves. Pride kept them from being in accountable relationships. Pride comes before a fall.

No man can mature when truth is absent. He isn't
pushed to be and to do his best. To become all God has
intended for us to be means we need to be accountable.

Accountability is like nuclear fusion. Everyone has
heard of it, everyone knows it's important, but very few
people actually know how to explain it. Here's a simple
definition: accountability means being "answerable on a
regular basis to qualified people for each of the key areas
of [one's] life."[2]

What does it mean to be answerable? It means to give
an accounting of our actions. When we are accountable
we choose to report how we are doing. To give a report
you need to be in relationship. You can't report to someone unless you have agreed to be in relationship and to
have accountability as part of your relationship.

We really do need each other. Where did we get this
idea of "every man for himself?" Rugged individualism
can isolate a man from friends who might alert him to
danger. The macho solo approach isn't biblical.

And we should not be afraid to ask other guys how
they are doing. As the apostle Paul wrote, "Each of you
should look not only to your own interests, but also to
the interests of others" (Philippians 2:4). We need to regularly be looking to the interests of each other. We need
to be courageous enough to ask the hard questions. Being a real man requires a friend who will walk alongside
us, speak the truth (even if it hurts), love us even when
we are blowing it, and challenge us to authenticity.

Second, be alone. Men who fall morally usually don't

have a friend to warn them. As I studied the lives of the men who fell into sexual sins, I discovered that each didn't have a friend who could say, "I think you better watch out." Or "I see some yellow lights—be cautious."

We all have blind spots. Friends who are committed to our growth can help us see foibles we didn't even know we had. A friend can alert you to dangers you can't see. Besides, having a friend is fun! It doesn't have to be only about accountability and keeping your promises. Sometimes you and I need a friend to be with and relax. It's an important part of understanding and developing the real man in each of us.

Third, be lazy. It takes work to be authentic. It takes effort to make our walk match our talk. In talking to some of the men who made poor moral choices, I discovered that some of them became lazy. And that can lead to becoming a fake guy.

"At first it was seemingly insignificant: coming in late, leaving early from work, taking longer lunches. Then it was fudging on my expense account. It was so much easier to take the shortcuts. Doing the ethical thing required so much effort."

Another guy had a similar experience.

"I was bored with my routine. I wanted to experience something new, but I didn't want to work at it. I didn't want to work on making my marriage more exciting. I didn't want to strive to build my relationship with my kids. That is why the affair was so easy. It was exciting and effortless. I fell into it."

"Fell" is the operative word. It doesn't take much effort for us to fall. Gravity does most of the work. All it takes for a man to fall is something to trip on. A lazy man is vulnerable to falling morally because he isn't making the effort to stay alert and avoid the things that might trip him.

Fourth, lust after women. I have worked with youth for over twenty years. Every year guys ask me, "Tim, when does a look become lust?" I have found it helpful to have discussions with young men about sexual attraction. I think we become more vulnerable when we don't have any venue to discuss sexual issues. I define lust as:

Living
Under
Sexual
Tension

Lust is the willful choice of allowing our natural sexual attraction to get a grip on us and trap us in sexual tension. Our focus becomes sexual lust.

As men, we notice gorgeous women. We like looking at attractive women. When does looking become lusting? When we take that second, lingering look. I have often counseled young men, "It's not wrong to enjoy the beauty of God's creation. You can look at a lovely lady and say, 'Now that's some creation! Thank God!' But we get into trouble when we move from admiring God's handiwork to wanting to touch it ourselves. I believe a look turns into lust when I begin to fantasize about the woman, wanting her for myself—wanting her sexually."

Just noticing isn't sin, but choosing to place ourselves under sexual tension is. Dwight L. Moody said, "It is not a sin to be tempted; the sin is to fall into temptation."

As Christian brothers, we can alert each other to snares that might trip us with lust. This is one way God provides for us to honestly deal with sexual attraction. God promises to help us during our temptations:

> So, if you think you are standing firm, be careful that you don't fall! No temptation has seized you except what is common to man. And God is faithful; he will not let you be tempted beyond what you can bear. But when you are tempted, he will also provide a way out that you can stand up under it. (1 Corinthians 10:12–13)

I believe that part of God's provision to help us handle sexual temptation is to be authentic with each other about our sexual tension. Scripture says temptation "is common to man." You are not alone. We gain power over sexual temptation when we are able to talk about it with other men. In silence and in solitude, sexual temptation can sneak up on you quietly, and destroy you before you know it.

One man nearly lost his marriage because of his lust. "I thought I was the only man who struggled with lust. I had never talked with anyone about my addiction to pornography. I was too ashamed. I was obsessed with it. It was ruining my family. Now, I have discovered liberty by admitting I have a problem. I am no longer ashamed. I am no longer alone. I have found many men who share my same problem. Together, with God's help, we are discovering a way out."

Fifth, be self-reliant. First Corinthians 10:12 contains a warning for the self-reliant man: "If you think you are standing firm, be careful that you don't fall." Success can make a man vulnerable to falling. He begins to rest on his accomplishments.

We are raised to be independent. Being the rugged, self-reliant man is part of our American heritage. "We would have never tamed the West if we had a bunch of sissies!"

Men typically want to control their own lives. Sometimes this drive can really work for us. Entrepreneurs must be independent, self-reliant men committed to a dream. But this pull to be independent can work against us. It can alienate us from God and other men. Independence rebels against the influence of God, as we think we can take care of ourselves. *I'll make it on my own* reasons the independent man.

A self-reliant man has difficulty being authentic. He has to maintain appearances at all costs. He can't afford to let down his guard—so he doesn't. His confidence is in his skills and resources. This can make him insecure. Deep down inside, the self-reliant man knows that he could lose it all—the achievement, the power and influence —all could be lost. It is a frightening possibility. Actually, it is a reality. The independent man will lose it all. When we die, we leave it all behind.

To be self-reliant we need power. But the power of a self-reliant man is an illusion. Real power originates from the hand of God.

The self-reliant man can easily forget about his Creator. He can begin to trust in his resources and in his own abilities. It can be a very unprotected position. As the prophet Jeremiah warns, "This is what the Lord says: 'Cursed is the one who trusts in man, who depends on flesh for his strength and whose heart turns away from the Lord'" (Jeremiah 17:5).

A real man can be authentic when he is dependent on the Lord. He doesn't have to be fake. He doesn't have to be a poser. He can be authentic because his value has been declared: "You are of inestimable worth. I have sent My Son to die for you. You are forgiven. You are My son."

A Christian man discovers his identity as a son because of the love of his heavenly Father. He can be secure in this identity because it can never be taken away from him. It survives unemployment. It is recession proof. It withstands anything that might happen.

SEEING OURSELVES AS WE REALLY ARE

To be authentic means to see ourselves as we really are. It means to be willing to look at ourselves the way that God sees us. Being authentic means admitting we need God to really understand ourselves. Without God's help, we are unable to understand ourselves. As Jeremiah wrote, we deceive ourselves: "The heart is deceitful above all things and beyond cure. Who can understand it?" (Jeremiah 17:9).

Guys who are willing to see themselves as God sees them are also more willing to be authentic with each other.

When we come to the Cross, we are all on level ground. The common ground at the Cross allows us to be authentic with each other. We can be genuine as we reveal what is on our hearts.

Your personality isn't the real you. The real you is the you that is known by God. When we are authentic with each other about our real selves, we can enjoy the company of genuine guys.

The man who depends on the Lord can be authentic and confident. Not because he knows or has everything—but because his Father does! Such a man, whose trust is in God, can be confident. As Jeremiah wrote, "Blessed is the man who trusts in the Lord, whose confidence is in him" (17:7).

Guidelines for Real Guys

Principle 2: A real guy can be authentic because his confidence is in the Lord, not in his natural strengths.

3

Is *Integrity* a Car?

*W*e hear a lot about being a "man of integrity." I see the phrase inscribed on men's hats, shirts, and key chains. If I didn't know that much about the Christian men's movement, I would assume that it had much to do with menswear and accessories.

Speaking of accessories, why do we have so few? Women have all kinds of stuff they can purchase to accessorize, but we're stuck with bland and boring things—like ties and (yawn) cuff links.

Of course, maybe it is better that we don't have a lot of accessories. We can get dressed faster. I have never heard a man say, "I will be there in a minute, honey. I just need to accessorize." (I'm not sure I *ever* want to hear that.)

Now, you may have "men of integrity" on your shirt, but do you have integrity in your heart? Do you know what it means? Is *integrity* a car? No, wait . . . that's *Integra*, by Acura.

INTEGRITY 101

So what does *integrity* mean? Don't worry; I'm not sure either. You might think a guy who went to a Christian university, graduated from seminary, and has hung around the church for twenty years would have a clear understanding of integrity, but I don't. Maybe it is because it seems old-fashioned or dated. Not too many TV shows or movies are promoting the virtue of integrity. So maybe you are like me—you have the shirt, but you aren't sure what the slogan means. Let's spend a few minutes with the basics. Pack your school bag; we are heading for class and a key course called Integrity 101.

According to Merriam Webster's Collegiate Dictionary (tenth edition), *integrity* means a "firm adherence to a code of especially moral values; soundness; completeness." Integrity implies trustworthiness and incorruptibility to a degree that one is incapable of being false to a trust, responsibility, or pledge.

Wow! OK, now I know why I haven't heard too much about integrity! It is an endangered species! Can you imagine being trusted to the point that people believe that you are incapable of breaking their confidence in you? I want people to say, "Not Tim! He could never do that! You must have the wrong guy or the wrong information." I think that is what Scripture means when it says "a man whose life cannot be spoken against" (1 Timothy 3:2 NLT). That verse could describe a guy of integrity —someone whose life cannot be spoken against.

Another reason we may not have a clear understanding of integrity is that Scripture uses several words to capture the idea of the English word, *integrity*. One of those colorful words is *blameless*. The underlying concept of blamelessness is that of completeness, or soundness. The complete truth involves telling all, honestly and correctly. Moral completeness involves a life that is upright and ethically sound. A guy with integrity lives a life that cannot be spoken against.

Another word in Scripture used to convey integrity is *upright*. Coming from the Hebrew language and culture, *upright* literally means *straight* or *level*. When a guy is level with his integrity we say "he is shooting straight." The upright man remains loyal to his commitments. He keeps his promises to people and to God.

A third word used in Scripture to describe integrity is

truthfulness. Integrity is walking in truthfulness. A guy of integrity will tell the whole truth. He won't hold back to protect himself. He is complete in his truth. He doesn't keep truth assigned to certain areas of his life. He allows truth to infiltrate every corner of his life. A guy of integrity wants the whole truth, so help him God.

Integrity is walking in truth. It is the relentless pursuit of that which is reliable and real. Integrity also captures the idea of being sound and complete. It comes from the same root word, which means *whole.* If we are men of integrity, we will be whole and complete because we are living in truth and committed to it.

SOUND ADVICE

I lived on an island in the Caribbean for a year. Roatan Island is a tropical paradise just off the coast of Honduras. I was there as a missionary, teaching local high school students. When I wasn't teaching, we went diving in the clear, warm waters; we would swim with colorful schools of fish, the bright orange coral our backdrop. It was a difficult job, but somebody had to do it.

One day I was talking to one of my islander friends about a boat. "How about that one in dry dock? It looks like it's in good shape, nice paint and no rust."

"Nah, she ain't no good."

"What do you mean?"

"No botta, she no good. Jest paint; no make no boat."

"The chrome is shiny, and the outboard looks new."

"Yah, mon, but you look at de wrong ting."

"She looks good to me."

"Yah, I know. Ya gotta look deep, mon."

"You can't judge a boat by its looks?"

"Yah gotta know a boat to know it."

It sounded like nonsense, but I asked, "How do you know a boat?"

"Every boat has a story. Yah listen to its story, you know de boat."

"What is this boat's story?"

"De paint tries to hide her story."

"You mean it is covering up something?"

"Dat's what I'm tellin' ya, mon. Dis boat ain't *sound!*"

"Sound? What's that mean?"

"A sound boat means it's all together. No hidden cracks in de hull, no surprises. Dis one is jest paint covering a hull dat is bustin' at de seams. She hold no water. You go out in her and she go down like a halibut."

"A sound boat is one that is strong on the inside and the outside," I said, trying to paraphrase what my island friend was saying. "It is consistent all the way through. A sound boat is seaworthy—you can risk your life with it."

"Yah, mon! Dat's what I tell you!" he exclaimed with annoyance.

My boat expert had expressed a fundamental principle that applies to people as well as ocean craft. We need to be sound—consistent through and through. As David said about his Lord, "Surely you desire truth in the inner parts; you teach me wisdom in the inmost place" (Psalm 51:6).

Are you like that old boat with a cracked hull? Are you coming apart at the seams but have disguised it with paint? Are you the same through and through? Or are you covering up something? Our lives are like boats; they need to be sound.

BEING STRONG ON THE INSIDE

To be effective and real as men, we must always focus on what's inside—on the internals and not the externals (like clothes, accessories, and achievement). Jesus was very much an inside-out kind of a man. Jesus sent his guys on a mission. He told them to travel light. "Do not take a purse or bag or sandals; and do not greet anyone on the road" (Luke 10:4).

Why did Jesus tell his seventy-two followers to travel light?

Because he wanted them to trust in Him, not in their stuff. He wanted to teach them that true security comes in knowing Him, not in being comfortable with their gear. Jesus didn't want His followers burdened with unnecessary loads. Notice that the fishermen left their nets, and the carpenters didn't carry their toolboxes. Jesus didn't want their vocational skills and tools to get in the way of the mission. In fact, Jesus told the seventy-two to not even carry a bag. He didn't want them trusting in their own abilities to provide for themselves. He wanted them to trust entirely on His provision. By leaving the extra pair of sandals they were indicating their obedience even if it was uncomfortable. Obedience isn't always comfortable.

Jesus also instructed His disciples to "not greet anyone on the road." He wanted them focused on the mission—telling others about His salvation. Jesus didn't want his followers getting sidetracked by pointless social conversations.

Christ's commands were necessary. They were vital to communicating the Good News in a speedy and effective manner. Can you imagine if the disciples didn't follow Christ's commands? Peter might have brought a pack burro with all of his stuff. Andrew might have brought a friend along to keep him company. Thomas would have hired a team of consultants.

Jesus told them to pack light because He wanted them to be ready and responsive for the journey. Jesus told them to travel light because He wanted them to focus on the internals, not the externals. Jesus modeled the man who is strong on the inside. Consider Laurie Beth Jones's observation in her best-seller, *Jesus CEO:*

> Jesus said, "Why do you seek after people's approval but do not seek the approval that comes from only God?" (John 12:42–43). He was an effective leader because he had internal anchors. He did not get his approval from external mechanisms. His actions were not based on what Peter, John and James thought. He didn't come unglued when John the Bap-

tist began to doubt him. He didn't care whether Caesar smiled or frowned.[1]

Guys of integrity aren't victims to the whims of the crowd. They have internal anchors that keep them grounded and centered. They have discovered that reputation is what people think about us, but character is what God knows we are.

LIVING BY OUR CONSCIENCE

"The most important thing in acting is honesty," comedy actor George Burns once said. "If you can fake that, you've got it made." As guys, we spend a lot of time trying to fake out each other. We spend much of our lives acting. We look to others for their approval and even their applause. We can easily become externally driven, instead of internally controlled. We may come to perceive that circumstances or other people are responsible for the quality of our lives. But this is a delusion. We are responsible for our choices. God holds us accountable for the decisions we make (not someone else).

Some of these decisions may seem small and insignificant at the time, but like tiny drops of rain, when they join together in a lifetime of choices, they can add up to a torrent that will affect our future. Over a few decades, our choices shape our character, and our character determines the quality and destiny of our lives.

Blaming others for our own poor decisions is one way we deal with an inconsistent life, one in which we don't live by our conscience. According to theologian Lawrence Richards, "When we don't listen to or live by our conscience, we tend to blame and accuse other people in an attempt to justify our own inner dissonance. If we don't have a sense of mission and principles to measure ourselves against, we benchmark against other people instead of our own potential."[2]

Scripture warns us to protect our conscience and to

listen to it. It is our God-given guidance system. In the
Old Testament, our conscience is referred to as our
"heart." "Above all else, guard your heart, for it is the
wellspring of life" (Proverbs 4:23).

Why would we need to guard our heart? Because we
tend to chase after our affections. If you subscribe to car
and racing magazines, watch stock car races on TV every
weekend, and have posters of your racing heroes in your
garage, it's just a matter of time before your affection for
racing causes you to bail on the Saturday yard work and
go to a race. We tend to act out our affections.

(Attention, Race Fans! I am not saying racing or attending races is sinful, so put your pneumatic wrenches
down.)

If our hearts are set on the right things, they will influence our behavior toward good. If our hearts are focused on evil or foolish things, they will prompt us
toward evil and foolish behavior. That is why we need to
guard our heart—it is the valve that lets out what we
have been tapping into. If we have been tapping into a
sewer, we can expect sewage. If we have been tapping
into Living Water, we can expect to see a "wellspring of
life."

A guy of integrity will seek to have a clear conscience.
He will take the extra effort needed to "maintain a clear
conscience before God and everyone else" (Acts 24:16
NLT). Walking in integrity means walking in truth before
God and others. People are likely to notice. They may ask
questions; they might tease you. Do you know what you
should do?

> If you are asked about your Christian hope, always be ready
> to explain it. But you must do this in a gentle and respectful
> way. Keep your conscience clear. Then if people speak evil
> against you, they will be ashamed when they see what a good
> life you live because you belong to Christ. (1 Peter 3:15–16
> NLT)

Those words from the apostle Peter are a recipe for freedom. If I am a guy of integrity, I don't have to worry about someone bringing up some dirt on me. I have no secrets. I don't have to "come out of the closet" with anything. My conscience is clear. I can stare my opponents in the eye and say, "Fire away. I have nothing to hide!"

I find it comforting to read "they will be ashamed." Their efforts to malign me will fail, because I am a man of integrity. Integrity provides great liberty.

A guy with integrity will have the courage to swim upstream. He won't always have to go with the flow downstream. He will be distinctive. He will also be blameless.

Stephen Covey, best-selling author and leadership consultant, reminds us of other benefits of listening to our conscience:

> People who listen to and live by their conscience . . . experience deep fulfillment—even in the midst of difficulties and challenges—and they go to bed at night with the confidence that they've done the most important things they could have done that day. They experience a deep level of inner peace and quality of life. They do not waste time rationalizing, fighting themselves, blaming and accusing other people or extrinsic conditions for their own situation. They have an almost sacred sense of stewardship about their roles—a sense of being "response-able" to contribute to quality of life for others in meaningful ways. They're strong in hard moments.[3]

"He was strong in hard moments." Don't you want that said of you? Having integrity means having the courage to do the right thing, even if it costs you more time, money, and effort. Maybe we are the strongest when we look at an opportunity to compromise our values and, in that moment of decision, make a commitment to principle—to walk in truth.

THE INCORRUPTIBLE FELON

Charles Colson was special counsel to President Richard Nixon. He had the president's ear. He was in a position of influence and notoriety. He went to Washington determined to set an example of clean government. His attitude was one of self-assurance and personal determination:

> No one was going to corrupt me. I had studied in college about Kant's categorical imperative: "Act as if the maxim of thy act were to become by thy will a universal law of nature." Heady stuff, and I swallowed it hook, line and maxim. I truly believed that with my intelligence, experience, and will, I could remain above reproach. I imagined that I could promise myself to be an upstanding man—and would be that. There was no need to bring God or anyone else into it.
>
> I ended up going to jail.
>
> So much for the idea that through my own resources and the rational process, I not only knew what was right but would actually choose to do it. So much for Kant's categorical imperative. So much for the idea that I alone, unguided by God, could live a consistently good life. So much for self-righteousness. In fact, we are never in greater danger than when we're self-righteous. [4]

While in prison, Charles Colson discovered a different resource for doing right: a personal relationship with Jesus Christ. When he was released, he founded an international ministry to prisoners, Prison Fellowship. After twenty years of consistent ministry, Colson has been recognized with honors for outstanding work in religion, including receiving the Templeton Prize in religion. Yet he still maintains a humble and dependent attitude; living out his words, "we are never in greater danger than when we are self-righteous."

INTEGRITY AND HUMILITY

We need to give up the notion that we can be good enough without God. We cannot be moving toward integrity in our lives without God's help. We cannot grow integrity in our souls with our own resources. We can't think hard enough or be disciplined enough to produce integrity on our own. To become men of integrity, we need to humbly come to God and ask for His help. As long as we are trusting in our own resources we cannot know God or become like Him. Integrity begins with humility and honesty. Consider James 4:6–8, 10:

> "God opposes the proud but gives grace to the humble." Submit yourselves, then, to God. Resist the devil, and he will flee from you. Come near to God and he will come near to you. Wash your hands, you sinners, and purify your hearts, you double-minded . . . Humble yourselves before the Lord, and he will lift you up.

Do you need to be lifted up? Could you benefit from a purified heart? Are you confused? Is your mind split over an issue? A person of integrity has a unified, whole mind—it isn't conflicted due to duplicity. Humble yourself before God.

Integrity is possible for guys like us, with all our failings, because of repentance. Repentance means going in the opposite direction. It means to do an about-face. The moment we realize that we have grieved God and His standard, we need to stop, confess our sin, and change direction. We can do this three, four, or seventy-seven times a day. A repentant heart is critical for effective Christian living and developing integrity.

When I was a young Christian, my discipler told me, "Keep short accounts with God. As soon as you sense you are out of step with Him, get back in step. Don't wait until the end of the day, at bedtime, and recite a long list of forgive-me's. Keep current with Christ throughout the day."

Repentance keeps our relationship with Christ close, current, and authentic. Close to Him so we won't stray. Current with Him so we have the strength to deal with today. And authentic before Him so we can be who He made us to be.

Close. Current. Authentic. That sounds like a guy of integrity.

Guidelines for Real Guys

Principle 3: A real guy is consistent inside and out, a mark of his integrity.

4
Wimp or Warrior?

I learned early in life that to be a man I must be a warrior. I was ten when I was in the army. OK, it wasn't the real U.S. Army, but it was real to us. We were the "Oswego Battalion," aptly named for the street we lived on in Aurora, Colorado. My next-door neighbor and friend, Leif, and my brothers, Danny and Joey, and a few of their buddies made up the core of the gang.

The incoming jetliners' approach lights lighted up our bedrooms at night. The planes were close, only a couple hundred feet above. Every ninety seconds (during peak hours) a jet would fly over our tri-level brick home on its way to land at Stapleton International Airport. This made for an exciting preadolescent transition for us boys.

It didn't take much to key us up. We were always ready for a battle, especially a pointless one. Our testosterone must have been hypercharged by the screaming of the jet engines, the shaking of the roof, and the blinding lights piercing the darkness at 3 A.M.

The ambience added a militaristic edge to our war games. We donned dark parkas, knit caps with the face (you know, the kind bank robbers wear), and dark gloves and jeans. We were camouflaged against the night. This was serious. This was war. Our weapons of choice were Benjamin Pump pellet guns. The more you pumped, the more velocity for the bullets. Instead of using the standard metal pellets, we discovered some chalk pellets (designed for indoor target practice) and used them for our battles. That is why we had to wear dark clothes. Chalk doesn't show up too well on white. Besides, it looks sissy.

THE OSWEGO BATTALION VS. THE PANSIES

The Oswego Battalion often challenged the wimps from the other street to a war in the emergency landing fields at the end of our street. To prepare for battle, we had built hideouts, bunkers, and foxholes. This was serious business; it required our focus and determination. It demanded that we stack the odds in our favor.

We often fought the Pansies. That wasn't their name, but that is what we called them. I think they actually called themselves the Peoria Panthers, but it didn't matter; we called them Pansies. It stuck. Why? Because we usually beat the little Pansies. Not that it matters now, of course. After the requisite name-calling and references to sisters, the war began. The Pansies would line up near the street and come across the field toward the Oswego Battalion.

This was our strategy. Earlier in the day, we had dug holes and covered them with burlap, leaves, and dirt. The Pansies couldn't see these at dusk. We waited in our foxholes and bunkers: snickering, peaking, and trying not to laugh and give away our hiding spot. We could laugh when a jetliner cruised in, seventy feet above our heads, the deafening howl of the engines covering our laughter.

A huge TWA jet swayed above. The Pansies charged with their flashlights and rifles. Would they see the trap? Would they fall in?

Stevie, our least-favorite Pansie, was the first to reach a pit. As he approached it, we let out a hoot: He didn't see it! He raised his rifle and aimed it toward the giggling in our bunker. But before Stevie reached the pit, he spotted us! We were within range of his rifle. Would he hit us? Points were scored by how many chalk marks were on the enemy. You weren't allowed to erase them (the chalk marks, not the enemy). If you did, you were considered "dead" and all of your "hits" didn't count.

Stevie charged forward, pumping his rifle. Just as he raised it to get us in his sights, he disappeared. He fell into the five-foot hole we had dug!

He wasn't hurt, just humiliated. It was a very gratifying moment. All of the preparation, all of the sweat, the digging, the planning, and the waiting were worth it. We had proven that we weren't pansies—we were warriors.

Now, when I think about it, all I can hear is my mother's voice, "It's all fun and games until someone gets an eye shot out."

PLAYING ARMY

What is it about boys that makes them want to shoot each other? Take two girls and place them under a tree, and they will pretend it's a nice place to have a tea party. Take two boys and place them under the same tree, and in thirty seconds they will break off limbs and pretend they are automatic rifles—shooting each other and making noises.

"Bamm, bamm, bamm! I got you!"

"I got you first! Bamm, bamm, bamm! You're dead!"

Why do boys like to play army? Could it be because we were designed by our Creator to be warriors? Is it OK for a Christian man to be a warrior? Or are we to be mild and passive advocates of peace?

What are we to be: wimp or warrior? Consider Gordon Dalbey's words in his best-seller, *Healing the Masculine Soul:*

The church has done much over the centuries to encourage men to pursue feminine virtues. But we have not sought and portrayed Christ-centered ways to pursue masculine virtues. It is not enough for Christians to portray weakness and tenderness as acceptable in a man. We also must portray the manly strength and firmness that is of God.[1]

We don't need to be afraid of our masculinity. We don't need to be embarrassed that we are men. Could it be that boys playing army are seeking to develop God-given tendencies to become mighty warriors for His kingdom? Can we embrace our masculine virtues instead of trying to feminize them?

Dalbey continues:

> We must demonstrate that weakness confessed and submitted to the Living God through Jesus Christ ultimately brings the very masculine strength for which men hunger: toughness in the face of opposition, decisiveness in the face of uncertainty, and saving power in the face of danger. . . . The work of God among men today—and so, the work of the Church—is not to feminize our masculinity, but to redeem it, not to make men more like women, but to make us more authentic men. [2]

FULLY MASCULINE

Authentic men have discovered their purpose. God has created men to be fully masculine—not partially masculine. Sure, some of us need to "get in touch with our feminine side," but we also need to get in touch with our masculine side. I like what Joseph Stowell, president of Moody Bible Institute, says:

> Many of us fear that if we fully yield the reins of our life to Christ, He will take away our manhood. Victims of a demasculinized portrait of Christ, we have forgotten that His perfect blend of divinity and humanity was expressed through existence as a man. He was the perfect expression of manhood. While that meant He had a special compassionate side, He also displayed strength and power. Enough strength and power to attract strong men as His followers. Enough so that they even gave up their careers and personal ambitions and followed Him.

Jesus Christ does not at all diminish our manhood. He emerges through the distinct qualities of our maleness to create a fuller and richer expression of what a man can be. He redefines our manhood by replacing the motivations of our world with new guidelines for success. He directs our manhood along the path of ultimate significance. He takes our instincts to protect, conquer, and accumulate, and points them in productive directions. [3]

Where did we get this idea that Jesus is a wimp? And to be like Jesus we need to be wimp-like? When a guy meets Jesus Christ, he is encountering God. Jesus is God, and He always has been. At the same time, Jesus is fully man. As a guy gets to know Jesus, he discovers a real man, a masculine man, one who faced all of life's challenges, temptations, and problems, and conquered them all. Jesus was no wimp. He was a man on a mission.

As we get to know Jesus, we discover that He does not diminish our manhood; He helps us discover it. Our maleness takes on its God-designed fullness and depth. Masculinity is a healthy and natural expression of God's design. A guy does not destroy his masculinity by giving up his macho pretense; he enhances it. A macho man has a tainted masculinity. His behaviors are a masquerade, hiding his insecurity and fear. The authentic masculine guy embraces the uniqueness of who he is in Jesus Christ and is devoted to working on the underdeveloped areas of his life.

But it is risky. We can be misunderstood as we develop both the tough and tender elements of our masculinity. Consider Norm Wright's observation:

To risk being different is to invite ridicule. The loss of status in the eyes of other men is a fear that can limit progress. There is also the fear, "I'll lose my masculinity. I'll be soft, passive, a pushover." No, the calling to be a Christian man is anything but soft and passive. Christianity embodies all of the genuine male characteristics in a balanced and healthy way. Man becomes more masculine in Christ, not less.[4]

That is powerful stuff: "Man becomes more masculine in Christ, not less." Perhaps this is what the apostle Paul had in mind when he presented his balanced view of masculinity. He was tough and tender. Let's consider his exercise of masculine virtue:

> Are they servants of Christ? (I am out of my mind to talk like this.) I am more. I have worked much harder, been in prison more frequently, been flogged more severely, and been exposed to death again and again. Five times I received from the Jews the forty lashes minus one. Three times I was beaten with rods, once I was stoned, three times I was shipwrecked, I spent a night and a day in the open sea, I have been constantly on the move. I have been in danger from rivers, in danger from bandits, in danger from my own countrymen, in danger from Gentiles; in danger in the city, in danger in the country, in danger at sea; and in danger from false brothers. I have labored and toiled and have often gone without sleep; I have known hunger and thirst and have often gone without food; I have been cold and naked. If I must boast, I will boast of the things that show my weakness. (2 Corinthians 11:23–27, 30)

After reading this list I know one thing: I don't want to hang around Paul! This guy was a walking calamity. He was a traveling lightning rod. Wherever he went, lightning and thunder struck.

Imagine that you are on a cruise. You know, the really fancy ones where you can eat enough food to feed a small Third World country. How would you like to discover that Paul was on board? I mean, this guy had a habit of causing shipwrecks. Three times! That has to be some kind of record.

Paul had to be tough. Jail. Physical abuse. Floods. Robbery. Betrayal. Hunger. Enemies at every turn. Paul had been tough in his pre-Christian days—when he was hunting and torturing Christians. When God redeemed Paul, the apostle had a redeemed masculinity. God didn't make him a wimpy, weak, passive spectator. God redirected Paul's warrior instinct toward being a warrior for His kingdom. God doesn't need wimpy males; he needs men who are tough and tender. God wants balanced men.

THE NURTURING WARRIOR

Consider Paul's balanced side (his more "feminine side"). He was tender as well: "As apostles of Christ we certainly had a right to make some demands of you, but we were as gentle among you as a mother feeding and caring for her own children. We loved you so much that we gave you not only God's Good News but our own lives, too" (1 Thessalonians 2:7–8 NLT).

What could be more tender than the image of a mother tenderly nursing her infant? The baby is totally dependent on the mother. The mother is patient and focused, not harried or distracted. Other chores can wait. The priority at hand is nurturing this child.

This is the same Paul who often checked out the city jail when he came to town because he knew sooner or later he would wind up there. Paul understood that we can be fully man and still tender. In fact, if we aren't tender, we aren't fully man.

Balance is evident in this Scripture. Note the last sentence, "We loved you so much that we gave you not only God's Good News but our own lives, too." It's not enough to deliver the goods and finish the task; we need to give of ourselves. Being an authentic man of God isn't simply handing out the gospel, it's living it and sacrificing our own lives. As men, we tend to focus on task more than relationship. In this Scripture, Paul helps us see the value of both. We need to complete the mission (share God's good news), but we also need to build relationships and share our lives with others.

Back to the analogy of the nursing mother. She is accomplishing a task (feeding her child), but she is also building a relationship. She is bonding with her baby.

Real men aren't afraid to balance responsibility with relationship. It's a battle, but that's why you are a warrior.

THE WEEPING WARRIOR

I used to joke about it in Sunday school. I thought it
was pretty funny then, in sixth grade. Our teacher would
ask, "What is your favorite verse?" Some of the kiss-ups
would preface their recitation by adding, "This is my life
verse." One day she asked me, "Tim, what is your verse?"

"John 11:35 is my verse," I quipped, "the shortest
verse in the Bible. Would you like me to recite it?"

"Yes, please," she responded politely.

"Jesus wept." I smirked, kids laughed.

I meant it as a joke (plus it saved me from memoriz-
ing Leviticus 15), but I have discovered that there is a
whole theology in that tiny verse. Maybe I wasn't so
tweaked in sixth grade after all!

When Jesus wept at his friend's grave, everyone there
saw His tears as a sign of His love, not of His weakness.
His affection for His dear friend and coworker, Lazarus,
was easily demonstrated with tears.

"Jesus wept."

In Sunday school we learned, "God is love." Jesus
demonstrated that He was God when He cried over the
loss of a friend.

"Love is God."

With that same power, of being authentic with emotions, Jesus raised Lazarus from the dead. Tough and
tender. Tender enough to cry, tough enough to beat death
at its own game.

We may be most like Jesus when we cry. Crying
makes us vulnerable. It also makes us real. "No human
response causes us to let go of our defenses more completely than heartfelt crying," Dalbey explains. "Therefore no response so hospitably invites the power of God,
and thereby threatens the Enemy."[5]

We can be weeping warriors. Our tears challenge Satan's attempt to put a stranglehold on men. He seeks to trap us with the "big boys don't cry" lie. When we grow up a little, we hear the "real men don't show emotion" myth. Both come from the pit. Our enemy doesn't want us to cry. He doesn't want us in touch with the reality of our emotions. Satan is the deceiver; he wants us faking ourselves out about our feelings. When we allow ourselves to cry, when we need to, we are actually doing battle with the enemy of Christ.

The "real men don't cry" lie has taken its toll on guys. It has cut us off from ourselves, from other men and women, and has distanced us from our Father God.

When was the last time you cried? As we grow closer to God, we grow in our compassion for others. Our heart is broken with the things that break the heart of God.

"I weep for the hurt of my people," Jeremiah wrote. "I am stunned and silent, mute with grief" (8:21 NLT). Jeremiah is known as "the weeping prophet"; his heart was so in touch with God's that he cried when he saw the callousness and wickedness of God's people. It broke his heart.

What breaks your heart? Are they the same things that break God's heart?

God's heart is broken by alienation and rebellion. He made us to have a relationship with Him, and His heart is broken when we harm that relationship. He grieves when we act without Him, when we don't include Him, when we intentionally leave Him out. Many men act as if they aren't broken, or capable of being broken; they are the most dangerous. Their pride (covering their fear) leads to self-deception. They aren't comfortable with the idea of their own woundedness. They are misguided warriors, seeking to conquer a foe, while they still haven't conquered themselves. True masculinity isn't about conquering a woman or another man; it's about conquering ourselves. It's defeating our built-in tendency to do it ourselves. It's admitting that we really do need someone else. It's looking deep into our soul and coming to grips with the fact that we really do need a Guide, a Mentor, and a Father.

"Authentic manhood can be approached only in relationship with the Father God, who seeks in every man to fulfill the purpose for which He has created him," Dalbey writes. "True manhood is not something to be sought, but to be revealed, precisely as a man submits to the God who called him into being and in whom lies his ultimate destiny."[6]

Perhaps the first step in becoming a true man is toward the Cross. At the Cross we shed tears revealing our brokenness and need for forgiveness. At the Cross of Christ we can be real about our wounds. No pretending. No positioning. At the Cross we discover our Father who longs to be with us. He invites us to release our self-centered pattern of living.

Tears at the Cross are a sign of true manhood. Those tears don't show that we are weak; they are a sign that our defenses are down. We are trusting enough to be real. We can come into God's presence incomplete, broken, and needy. He sees us forgiven, healed, and willing to follow His lead.

Real men do cry. Some of the mightiest warriors do their battles on their knees, in small pools of tears. Tears of compassion and intercession for others. Tears of joy as whole men who are forgiven and empowered to love our families and our God.

Guidelines for Real Guys

Principle 4: A real guy has learned to be tough and tender.

5
Men Are from Mars, Women Are from the Mall

I have just finished my exhaustive research for this chapter. In addition to watching forty-three episodes of *I Love Lucy*, I have read several of the best-sellers on men and women, including John Gray's insightful *Men Are from Mars, Women Are from Venus*. After hours of reading and a cash investment that rivals the gross national product of a Third World country, I am proud to share with you my insights about men and women:

Men and women are different.

Brilliant, isn't it?

Famous psychologists, smiling guys on infomercials, expensive seminar speakers, and best-selling authors try peddling it in their own style; but it basically comes down to this: "Women aren't like us guys." For some guys, it becomes quite an issue: "Women aren't like us guys—and it ticks us off!"

As the gentlemen asked in *My Fair Lady*, "Why can't a woman be like a man?" Or at least like a guy?

Because people are different.

I know what you are thinking, *Wow! Insights into the obvious. I have wasted my money on this book.* (I know the feeling.)

Women are not guys. They are different from us (and I am not just talking about their plumbing). We know this, but we spend a lot of time trying to change the reality of it. We think we can tweak the truth by pretending that women are just like guys, but with makeup.

In practice, many guys don't acknowledge that women are different. They resist and reject how women are different. They try treating them like guys. Many of these same guys are quite lonely for female companionship. When women don't feel, think, or behave like they want, these guys get angry or try to "fix them." This approach doesn't work. Have you noticed that women want our interest, not our improvements?

A BASIC DIFFERENCE:
TASKS VS. RELATIONSHIPS

That insightful observer of human behavior Tim Allen says, "Women are not the opposite sex, they're a whole other species."[1] Meanwhile John Gray has noted that women are from different planets than men. My conclusion? Men are from Mars, women are from the mall. Women savor the experience of shopping, but men want to complete the process. It's a key difference between the sexes: Men want to complete tasks and move on; women want to enjoy the experience and build on their relationship with their friends or family.

Women like to browse; that is why they love malls. They like to embrace the experience: the sights, the smells, and the possibilities. "How would I look in that skirt? Would it match the sweater I saw nine stores back?" Women enjoy doing this with a friend. This is important—they want their opinion.

"How do I look in these pants? Are they too tight in the back?"

"Yeah," grimaces her friend, truthfully, "they are a little snug." (Like two sizes too small.) A female friend can get away with this, but don't you dare try! This is a no-win situation. If you say, "Well, it's a bit tight," you hurt her feelings. If you say it's OK and she finds out later you thought it didn't fit well, she'll ask, "Why can't you tell me what you think? I want your honest opinion. Don't hold things from me."

Guys, of course, don't like to browse. Most of us don't like malls. "Just give me the kind of store I can park in front and run in and get what I need. You know, like a hardware store."

Guys don't care about the process of shopping; they want the product. They don't need to hang around, browse, and consider the possibilities. You won't hear guys musing in the mall, "I wonder if that yellow cable knit sweater I saw in Bloomingdale's will match this snappy outfit in Macy's?" They are more likely to ask, "Hey, where is the rack of jeans?"

Guys aren't interested in the experience; they want speed. My goal when I go to the mall is to park as close as possible to the *one* store I am going to shop in, rush in, buy the one thing I need, and get out. Guys don't mind doing this alone; in fact, they prefer it. I can't imagine a guy asking his friend to accompany him to browse the mall. I can't imagine a guy asking his friend, "Do these pants make me look big?" as he glances over his shoulder to check out his caboose.

This male-female difference regarding time and relationship is shown in preferences in movies and books. In general, men want action (and some violence) in movies and novels. Women want romance and relationships. A guy is happy if the movie has state-of-the-art special effects. A woman is happy if the movie has intimate dialogue and a male lead who completely understands the female lead (or is Mel Gibson, Leonardo DiCaprio, or Denzel Washington).

This is why it is difficult to choose a movie or video. Women want one thing out of a movie; men want something entirely different. Blockbuster movies have usually figured out a way to give both women and men what they want.

It isn't a problem for men and women to be different.

The problem comes when we try to change each other into revised editions of ourselves. It is difficult to love someone we are intent on changing. Consider Gray's words:

> Real love is unconditional. It does not demand but affirms and values. Unconditional love is not possible without the recognition and acceptance of our differences. As long as we mistakenly believe that our loved ones would be better off thinking, feeling, and behaving the way we do, true love is obstructed. Once we realize that not only are people different but they are supposed to be that way, the obstacles to real love begin to fall away.[2]

ACCEPT AND EXPLORE

Two concepts that are critical to understanding and relating successfully to women are *accept* and *explore*. We must accept that all people are different and are supposed to be that way. Clearly women are different, and Gray says guys need to accept that their wives or girlfriends are going to be different from them. This allows us the possibility of growing unconditional love. We give up the notion of trying to change women and begin thinking about how to accept them unconditionally.

Accept means that we will receive willingly and approve. Women need men to receive them willingly, in spite of their differences. A woman looks for a man to embrace her for who she is, not how she does according to some checklist. When a woman feels accepted by a man, it gives her freedom.

Unconditional love communicates acceptance. Consider how freeing it is to another person when you can say:

"I accept you for who you are. I know you are different from me, but that is what I like. I want you to be who you are. You don't need to be like me. There may be times when we don't understand each other. There may

be days when the differences lead to conflict. But I want
you to know I love you unconditionally. I have committed myself to accepting you and exploring you. I want to
get to know you deeply. You don't need to be a certain
way for my approval. You don't need to act like me, feel
like me, or think like me. You can be yourself. I will always love you."

If you are married, you probably said a variation on
this theme in your marriage vows. Do you remember, "in
sickness and health, in poverty or riches, 'til death do us
part"? Marriage vows are formal declarations of unconditional love.

The second word that helps us understand unconditional love is *explore.* As men, this comes naturally. We
are hunters and gatherers. Exploring is second nature to
men. Go with it. Use your God-given, natural inclination
to explore with your woman (wife or girlfriend). I'm not
saying pack her on the dogsled and race the Iditerod. I
am thinking of exploring how she is different from you.
Hunt for what she likes. Gather this information and
store it in your mental teepee. A woman feels valued and
approved when a man seeks to explore and understand
her.

DEVELOPING UNCONDITIONAL LOVE

Accept and explore are two keys to developing unconditional love. And that is the love which Christ calls
us to and has for us:

> Love each other as I have loved you. Greater love has no one
> than this, that he lay down his life for his friends. You are my
> friends if you do what I command. I no longer call you ser-
> vants, because a servant does not know his master's business.
> Instead, I have called you friends, for everything that I
> learned from my Father I have made known to you. (John
> 15:12–15)

God accepts us. In spite of our belligerence and hard-headedness, He still loves us. He wants to have a relationship with us. That is why He sent Jesus—to restore the relationship. To pay the price of our indifference and rebellion. To build a bridge between God and people.

God accepts us in Christ. We don't have to become perfect or super spiritual. We simply need to come to Him. Isn't that what grace is all about? I like to define grace as "love in relationship." God loves us so much that He wants a relationship with us. He will go the greatest lengths to have that relationship, including sacrificing His own Son. Isn't that the greatest love—being willing to lay down what is valuable to us for another?

At weddings I like to share a definition to help the couple capture this idea of unconditional love: "Love is taking the initiative to act sacrificially to meet the needs of another."

Love isn't afraid to make the first move. Love is courageous enough to sacrifice. It isn't selfish or demanding. Love is alert to know what the other needs.

To know what our wives need, we need to be explorers. We need to invest the time and the effort to get to know our wives well enough to know what their needs are. This may involve not watching the ball game (sacrifice). This may require getting out of your recliner (initiative). It may also require you to think about your wife in a new way. Remember, she is your friend, not your servant. We treat our wives like servants when we expect them to know what we like and to conform to it.

"Hey, how come my dinner isn't on the table when I come home from work? What have you been doing?" (It may be hard to believe, but I have actually asked this!)

CONFIDING IN A FRIEND

Even Jesus doesn't treat us like servants (though He has a right to). He calls us "friends." We don't confide in servants. We confide in friends. We don't communicate on a deep level with servants. We do with friends. Confidence and communication are elements of a meaningful friendship.

Can you imagine trying to have these with a servant? OK, so most of us don't have servants; but imagine you are at the garage dropping your car off for repair. You speak to your mechanic:

"It's so good to see you, Frank. I know I haven't been in for a while. It's just that . . . well, the car, it hasn't needed to be fixed. Don't take it personally."

"What?"

"Just because I haven't been around doesn't mean I don't care."

"Huh?"

"I am so glad we can talk. Just between you and me, I am feeling inadequate. I just don't know if I can do it all."

"Fine. Just leave me the keys."

"Thanks for listening. I feel much better."

"Yeah, sure."

We don't confide in servants; we confide in friends. Here's a novel thought for some of us: Consider your wife your friend! Sometimes our expectations for our wives are shaped by viewing them as servants rather than friends. As men, it's easy to fall into that trap of "What have you done for me lately?" A guy's sense of self is defined through his ability to achieve results. We apply this same value to relationships. We value people for what they can do for us. Jesus values us, not for what we can do for Him, but because He loves us. He calls us "friends."

Friends meet each other's needs and demonstrate value to each other. A guy can actually be a friend to a woman—even his wife! He just needs to understand a few things. Recognize, for instance, that "men are motivated and empowered when they feel needed. . . . Women are motivated and empowered when they feel cherished."[3]

When a guy feels needed in a relationship, it energizes him to invest in the relationship. When a woman feels cared for and nurtured, she is motivated to bring her all to the relationship. Our needs are different, but complementary: guys need solutions, women need to express their feelings. Understanding these differences between the sexes will help. When a guy has a problem, he will retreat to focus on it until he can come up with a solution. Perhaps he will ask a trusted friend for advice. This consultation is designed to come up with a solution. When a woman faces a problem, she wants to share. She doesn't want to retreat to focus; she wants to talk about her feelings. The talking helps make sense of her feelings.

What we need out of a relationship will affect how we approach it. Guys might be looking for answers, but they may need affection. They might be tempted to "stay in their head" when they really need to get in touch with their feelings. Women may be looking for opportunities to relate and express their feelings; but they may really need to spend time thinking, prioritizing, and adding structure to their feelings.

"MENISMS": TRUTHS ABOUT MEN

In my research, which consists of many hours observing guys in their natural habitats—golf courses, sporting venues, and parked in their lounger in front of the game on TV—I have come to realize that most guys have five things in common. If you are aware of these five traits, it will help you comprehend, with perspicacity (this word has nothing to do with perspiring; it means "insight") how to have an effective and enjoyable relationship with women.

I call these five traits of men *menisms:* truths about our masculine soul that fundamentally affect our relationships with women.

1. *Men are never certain they have a relationship.* Women know if they have a relationship and even understand the varying degrees of relationship. Guys are often

clueless about the existence, quality, and level of commitment of a relationship with a woman. This includes married guys.

The message to each of us must be the same: "You have a relationship. Just because she is your wife doesn't mean she came with the house. She is a person of immense value. Get to know her!"

Women understand that they are in a relationship. Women often know on what level of intimacy the relationship rests. Men aren't sure. When they hear the word *intimacy,* they think of sex. Women also know what needs they have and how their man should meet them. Guys, on the other hand, expect that because they are in a relationship that should be enough; just being together should meet most of the women's needs, they reason. Guys expect there to be no more problems once they are in a relationship.

2. *Men are not afraid, unless you are talking about* commitment. I have seen 275-pound linebackers run scared when their five-foot-four, hundred-pound girlfriend started talking about the "C" word. It really got frightening when she started leafing through *Brides* magazine. *Commitment* means demonstrating courage in your relationship with your wife.

Are you courageous? Commitment to relationship may be tough for some of us, but it is crucial in being a real guy. We will explore how to develop committed relationships in chapter 8.

Women are more comfortable with commitment. In fact, they like it. Men are more comfortable with analysis and problem solving. Women are more comfortable with the experience and sharing feelings. It takes commitment to relationship to create an atmosphere for sharing. Women are good at this; that's why they like to "come over for tea" or "go out to lunch, just to catch up." I have yet to hear a guy call another guy and ask, "Will you join me for tea and croissants, just to catch up?"

3. *Men want to learn how to be more sensitive and in touch with their feelings.* Guys are open to developing their "feminine side"; but for some, it's just not a priority. Besides, most of us haven't seen too many examples of men who are sensitive and aware of their emotions. At least we haven't seen very many we want to be like. But that doesn't mean that guys are against the idea. They want to become more aware, though they are not sure how realistic it is; just like they like the idea of winning the lottery, even though they aren't sure how attainable it is.

Women are more at home with their feelings. They see them more as their allies. Guys distrust feelings. They are afraid of their power. Most men look at emotions like they are sleeping giants; better not to wake them. (More on that distrust and how to deal with it in the next chapter.)

Most women see their emotions as signals of what is going on in their world. They embrace their emotions. Most men hold their emotions at an arm's distance; straight-arming them to keep them from getting too close.

One suggestion for guys who are ready for change: You can start with telling your wife how you are feeling. Each day use a different word to describe your feeling (after all, our feelings change day to day). In a week, you will have seven choices of words to describe how you are feeling. For some guys, this is huge—they are used to grunting, "OK" when asked how they are doing.

4. *Men are interested in* communication *(as long as it doesn't interfere with the play-offs).* Women communicate differently than guys. Guys can bond around a play-off game and communicate affection with high fives, anger with banging the coffee table with their drink can, and elation with hoots and screams. It's a distinct form of communication:

"Ohh! Can you believe it? He was out of bounds! What is wrong with those refs?"

"Yeah, are they blind? They are clueless. Hey, pass the peanuts."

"Do you think they will play the new guy, what's-his-name?"

"Maybe. I mean they should—they pay him enough. WOW! Did you see that play?"

"Amazing. Want some more buffalo wings?"

"DUH! What a dumb play!"

"Yup"

"Man!"

"Arggh!"

"Dooph"

"Yikes"

"Sheesh"

Guys can communicate. They may not use a lot of words, but they can get the message across. I heard recently that men use about five thousand words in one day and women about twenty thousand. When a guy reaches his limit, he stops. (It's like fishing.) Some women expect guys to communicate like they do (using a lot of words). Part of the difference is women are more verbal; even as children, females are more verbal than men, studies show. They have more ability for extended conversation than their male counterparts. Women have more words to use in one day. They are much more fulfilled when they get to use most of their words.

Guys, in contrast, are happy if they are not challenged to do more than their limit. They are content to save their words.

"Honey, please pass the chips."

"Have you seen the remote?"

"When did you dye your hair red? Was it during football season?"

Of course, some women try to communicate with their husbands during the play-offs. This is destined to fail. Timing is everything.

5. *Men are looking for a challenge (especially a point-*

less one). Guys have a built-in device called a "Dare-ome-ter." When someone challenges them, the dare-ometer kicks in and warns the guy, "Ready Alert—you have been challenged. Stand by for action!"

The challenge may be dangerous, senseless, and even pointless; it doesn't matter. If a guy is challenged, he must respond. I think this explains a lot of the cases in the emergency rooms of local hospitals.

Women don't go looking for senseless challenges. I can prove it to you. Most of those "Funniest Home Video" TV shows feature guys doing dumb stuff, not women. If they show women, it's usually because she got caught, as an innocent bystander, in some guy's hare-brained stunt. Women are much more interested in being real. Guys like to pretend that they are superheroes, stunt men, or professional athletes. Women prefer the challenge of being authentic, sharing feelings, thoughts, and needs. Guys would rather ride a motorcycle through a circle of fire than do that.

Basically, guys like to compete, and women like to cooperate. Because we are different, one of the biggest challenges we have is to love someone who is so different from us. We can take this on as a challenge, but it won't be a pointless one. We can even make it a competition, if it helps: learning to love our wives in such a way that we defeat the seeds of divorce.

Guidelines for Real Guys

Principle 5: A real guy demonstrates love by accepting differences in a relationship and acting to meet the needs of the other person.

6
Feelings—
Can You Trust Them?

*F*eelings are scary—they are unpredictable. Probably one of the most embarrassing things for a guy is to get emotional in the wrong situation. I'm thinking here of an annual athletic awards banquet in my high school years ago. The following story is true; the names have been changed to protect the innocent (and not-so-innocent). It happened at San Clemente High School in southern California.

"Now it's time for the Most Inspirational Award," Coach Reese announced. "This is an important award to me as a coach, because I need inspiration. I mean, sometimes it's difficult to motivate these guys to train for cross-country. I'm always looking for inspiration."

Those words came from the coach who liked to drive his sports car beside us and yell, "Pick up the pace! You're loafin'!" It made us want to chuck rocks at him as he drove by.

Coach continued: "The inspirational award goes to the athlete who has distinguished himself by supporting the team and keeping us going. It's about motivation. I am proud to announce this year's Most Inspirational Award goes to Chris Kearins."

We were surprised. Chris was a consistent runner—consistently slow. But he had a steadiness that gave us strength. He wasn't flashy, but predictable; we could always count on Chris. He worked hard at practice and gave his all at meets. We thought Coach would have picked Peter Brandes, the outgoing, flamboyant, cheerleader comic that kept us in stitches. Instead, Coach chose Chris. We were overwhelmed; so was Chris.

Chris stumbled out of his chair, dumbfounded. Applause broke out as he walked across the cafeteria floor. Peter jumped up on his chair and started hooting. He didn't seem bothered that he wasn't selected. Chris tripped on the last step on the stage. He turned toward the audience, which broke out in an uproarious laugh.

Coach shook Chris's hand and presented him with the trophy. With a pat on his back, Coach stepped back and gestured to the podium. Reluctantly, Chris stepped forward, fiddled with the microphone (making it emit feedback), and cleared his throat.

"Uh . . . I'd like to, uh, thank Coach for this award. I am shocked. I wasn't expecting it."

Applause interrupted his speech.

"I didn't think I would get anything tonight, except the rubbery chicken."

People laughed.

"I feel so . . .I'm glad for this . . .ahh . . . I'm not even that fast . . . but I guess you consider me inspirational. I just wanted to be . . ." Chris paused and wiped a tear from his left eye. "I wanted to . . ." He started to choke up. His Adam's apple was going up and down trying to keep the tears down.

Coach shifted his weight. He was in plain view as he stood just a few feet behind Chris on the stage in the cafeteria. Coach looked uncomfortable with the level of emotion. He was always trying to be macho. Macho men don't cry, especially coaches; but Chris was getting to him.

"I came out for cross-country because it was the only sport I thought I could do. I stayed with it for two reasons: my teammates and Coach Reese. My teammates were always there for me, cheering me on, congratulating me even though I am not that fast. Thanks guys!" He wiped a tear from his eye and gestured toward us.

We hooted and clapped.

"And Coach," he continued, "what can you say about Coach?"

"He's an egomaniac dictator?" whispered Ralph. Everyone at our table laughed, even the parents.

"Coach believed in me when no one else would, including myself. Coach gave me a chance to prove something to others and myself. I learned that with discipline, perseverance, and encouragement from others, we can achieve. Coach has helped me achieve." He glanced at Coach and smiled gratefully. "Thanks, Coach!"

Coach lost it. He tried to maintain his macho aloofness, but he couldn't. Chris's words punctured his veneer. He reached into his coat pocket and pulled out a bandanna (I didn't think he owned a handkerchief.) He dabbed his eyes and blew his nose.

"Blaaughh!" It sounded like a foghorn. All eyes were now on Coach. Chris's next sentence was lost in the deafening blast and the aftershock. Coach was now bobbing up and down with emotion. He looked like those dogs people put in the rear window of their cars; the kind with springs that make the head bob when they hit a bump in the road.

"Look at Coach. He's crying!" whispered Ralph, a little too loud.

We watched with amazement. We had never seen Coach act this way. The only emotions we had seen in him were anger (usually at us) and pride (when we won, which wasn't too often). We had never seen him cry; after all real men don't cry.

THE MAN OF STEEL

The macho man likes to project that he is made of steel. He seeks to portray invulnerability. He is a man who can't be touched. He is a man in control and not subject to unpredictable emotions. Of course, most of this is pretending. But guys aren't the only ones who do this; animals do too. I guess you could call macho posturing animal behavior. That's what Tom Eisenman thinks:

> A peacock raises its tail feathers to scare off attackers. It is a behavior meant to disguise weakness and vulnerability. A turtle retreats into the dense defense of its shell. Men often behave like the peacock or the turtle. If we are in danger of being found out, we will fan our achievements and wield a display of power, or we will retreat into our impenetrable fortresses. Either way our manly image remains intact. We are proud creatures.[1]

The steel man seeks to avoid any exposure of his insecurities, fears, weaknesses, and vulnerability. His strength and capabilities shape so much of his identity. The steel man doesn't want to reveal his frailties because that would compromise his masculine identity. This, of course, is not true; but steel men believe in the I-must-be-tough-at-all-times myth.

As we noted in menism number three in the previous chapter, most men want to be in greater touch with their emotions; yet they also distrust their feelings. And most men soon become men of steel, wrongly assuming that real men don't show emotion. This lack of feeling is not what God has intended, according to professor and counselor Gary Oliver.

> By acting as if emotions and masculinity are incompatible, we have limited who God created us to be and become. The most devastating loss we have suffered by accepting these distortions is the loss of our hearts—the loss of our ability to feel, the ability to be tender as well as tough. We have lost the ability to be whole people.
>
> These myths have produced a generation of men who are significantly out of touch with what it means to have been created in the image of an infinite yet personal God. . . . Be-

cause men don't understand and know how to express their emotions, they don't know how to deal with emotional pain. Therefore, when we do have pain we don't understand it and don't know what to do with it, so our only option is to anesthetize it. If we don't feel, then we won't feel pain or fear or grief or loss. The anesthetic works for a while, but over time we need more and more. This leads to all kinds of destructive habits.[2]

Like the tin man in the *Wizard of Oz,* the steel man has no heart. He has lost it; he has lost part of his God-given ability to feel. He is not whole. He may be successful in achievement, but he is incomplete. He may be the only one who knows this about himself. He may have a persistent nagging that something is missing, but he can't put his finger on it. Those around him may see him as heartless and self-serving—that was Jack's problem.

JACK OF HEARTS

Jack is a successful executive. His abilities have brought him wealth and admiration in his business community. But Jack is not whole. He has lost the ability to be a whole person. He doesn't know how to understand and express his emotions. He doesn't know how to deal with emotional pain. Jack is emotionally disabled. He wasn't comfortable with emotions. He wasn't equipped to deal with pain.

Jack wanted a son. For years, he and his wife, Diane, tried to have a baby. After thousands of dollars and endless trips to specialists, Diane became pregnant. The ultrasound indicated a boy! Jack was elated. He had produced big business deals, but he had never produced a son. He was proud, excited, and anxious.

I received a call one afternoon. Diane was in the hospital and giving birth early to their son; would I come? I canceled my appointments and rushed to the hospital. I found Diane in a relatively positive mood in spite of the pain. Jack was still at work.

"He'll be here as soon as he can," explained Diane.

The pain increased with each hour. More and more hospital personnel were filing into the room. I had seen this before—the baby was in trouble. Diane's labor intensified, and Jack showed up just in time to see the birth of his son—stillborn.

Jack was mortified. This was not part of his plan. A dead child did not fit into his perfect world. He showed shock for a few minutes, then retreated to his shell. He was in danger of being found out. His vulnerability was exposed. He covered it quickly.

As the nurses attended his wife, I suggested we go grab a bite to eat. We had missed dinner and now noticed our gnawing hunger.

"Hey, Jack, let's go get a burrito. I know this great Mexican food place."

"Sure, I'm starved."

A few other close friends joined us. Jack ordered his burrito and Coke and sat down to munch the chips. "Pass me the salsa, please," he asked.

I looked at him with amazement; he was smiling and chomping. He was back in his shell. He was projecting the cool and in-control Jack. Forty-five minutes earlier he was expecting his firstborn son. Forty minutes earlier he discovered that his son was dead. Now it didn't seem to matter. At least, that was how he was acting.

"I'm really sorry for your loss, Jack," I offered.

He didn't respond to the expression of care. He wasn't comfortable with compassion. He didn't know how to handle emotion. He certainly didn't know what to do with grief. So he hid from it; he pretended everything was OK. It was the weirdest Mexican meal I had ever had. As I munched on my burrito, I kept thinking, *This is weird! Jack just lost his son, and it doesn't seem to faze him. Something is wrong; he is acting like his heart is made of steel.*

Jack was living out Norm Wright's assessment of men

and their feelings: "Men have learned clever techniques for withholding their feelings. The message they send to the world is that emotional expression and survival don't mix—and they believe it!"[3]

Jack never displayed grief, not even tears at his son's funeral. He has many things, but he doesn't have a whole heart.

FEELINGS GOT A BAD RAP

These are some of the slogans we hear. Do any sound familiar?

Big boys don't cry.
Real men don't get emotional.
Don't trust your feelings.
It's just weak people who are emotional.

I grew up with some of these mottoes ringing in my head. Several adults told me that I shouldn't cry. *But it feels right to cry.* I protested silently to myself. *It hurts, and crying makes me feel better.*

At church I was urged to not get too emotional. "It will lead to theological error," one youth pastor said.

At seminary I was taught to think, but I wasn't taught how to feel. I came out with an enlarged head and a shrunken heart. All of this taught me to distrust my emotions. In my experience, feelings were ignored or not regarded as important, sort of like second-class citizens. In some circles, feelings are taught against. This bothers me—did God make a mistake? Did He slip up for a few minutes in creating humans and mistakenly shape feelings into our design? I don't think so; God intentionally made us emotional beings. In fact, the Holy Spirit can prompt our emotions. His work isn't limited to working on our minds or will; He desires to impact our hearts.

We are created in His image. We have minds, wills, and hearts. As whole people, we have the capacity to feel and express our feelings. This makes us like God. Being emotional doesn't make you less of a man; it might make you more like God.

WHAT ABOUT TEARS?

Our emotions are important. We need to learn how to listen to them and understand them. I see emotions as gauges. In our cars we have gauges that tell us if the engine is running hot or needs oil. If we ignore these gauges, it could be trouble. Our emotions can tell us a lot about ourselves, if we heed their warning. Isn't it ironic that we are proud of our intellect, stubborn in our wills, but ashamed of our emotions? Something is wrong in our culture when men are affirmed and taken seriously because they don't share their feelings, and women are not taken seriously because they share their feelings.

As Charles Swindoll writes:

> Expressing one's emotions is not a mark of immaturity or carnality. The loss of a loved one is just as much a loss for the believer as it is for the nonbeliever. A killer disease like cancer —especially in its final stages—arouses the same feelings in the Christian's heart as in the heart without Christ. Pain is pain. Loss is loss. Death is death. At such times tears are not only acceptable, they are appropriate and expected. It is part of being real, being human.[4]

Jesus wept. At a time of loss, He demonstrated His true emotions. We don't think less of Him for doing this; we think more of Him.

Romans 12:15 (NLT) instructs us, "When others are happy, be happy with them. If they are sad, share their sorrow." How can we do that without getting emotional? According to this verse, to obey God we must get emotional.

The phone rang as I was writing this chapter, a call from the emergency room. A three-year-old girl had fall-en into a swimming pool. Her life was in the balance. "Would you come to be with the family?"

"Sure, I'll be there in a few minutes." I wasn't sure what I would say. What do you say to a mother whose child might die? I thought about my theological training. She didn't need a treatise on the sovereignty of God. I thought about my education in psychology. She didn't need to hear about the five stages of grief. I thought about my years of supervising children and youth. She didn't need my input on waterfront supervision. As I walked into the emergency room, the verse popped into my mind, "When others are happy, be happy with them. If they are sad, share their sorrow." I decided to not say much. Instead, I hugged the mother and cried with her.

Later, I offered a weepy prayer. I spent the night with the family in the waiting room. We chatted a little, but we cried a lot. The girl died in the morning. Later, the mother told me it was my tears that ministered to her.

Sometimes, to obey God, we must get emotional.

HOW TO BECOME A COMPLETE GUY

As guys, there are certain situations that we work hard at avoiding. Some of this is normal, but sometimes we spend a lot of energy running from our emotions. We seek to maintain control by maintaining distance. We avoid the uncomfortable emotions: fear, anger, embarrassment, loneliness, insecurity, feeling dumb, and feelings of failure.

How can we learn to feel more comfortable with our emotions? When we have a whole heart, we will experience so much more of life. When we begin to use our emotions instead of running from them, our lives will have a new vitality.

Here are seven suggestions to becoming the complete guy, free to express your emotions:

1. *Realize that God made you an emotional being. (It's OK, really!)* Seek to understand your emotions, rather than to fight or avoid them.
2. *Accept that women are wired differently emotionally.* You don't need to share your feelings like a woman. However, learn to hunt for your submerged feelings and be brave enough for intimacy.
3. *Enjoy the benefits of becoming aware and sharing your feelings.* It will provide you with a new set of relational tools.
4. *Tune into others, listening for clues to how they are doing emotionally.* In other words, read between the lines. Learn to read nonverbal cues.
5. *Expand your vocabulary to better express your feelings.* Instead of responding to your wife's question about your day with "fine," experiment with a wider choice of words that more accurately reflect how you really feel. For example, try *effective, worthwhile,* and *fun.* If it didn't go well, try *mad, confused, embarrassed,* etc. Become familiar with a thesaurus to discover new and more specific words to describe how you are feeling. Some guys find it helpful to use word pictures to describe how they feel. Word pictures are analogies that express your true feelings. "I felt like an Olympian, standing on the awards stand when I received that bonus today."
6. *Keep a journal.* Record what goes on in your life and how you feel about it. Try to be as specific as possible in your descriptions. Emphasize emotions more than simply recording the events of the day. For instance, "I was worried about the project at work. I am not sure if I have the resources to pull it off. I might be in over my head. Sometimes I feel like I am trying to swim with a hippopotamus on my back." (Now *that's* a word picture.)

7. *Make yourself accountable.* Ask your wife (or, if single, your girlfriend) and a couple of guys you can trust to hold you accountable to develop your emotional side. Let them know you are working on becoming more aware of and sharing your feelings. Give them permission to ask about your progress. Ask them to affirm any progress they observe. Let them know this is new for you, and it will take time to learn; any encouragement would be appreciated.

With support, acceptance, and appreciation, we have the motivation to change—to become the complete guy.

Guidelines for Real Guys

Principle 6: A real guy recognizes that his emotions are a God-given resource for understanding himself and connecting in relationships.

7
Gliders,
Softballs, and Referees

*E*nthusiastic men filled the stadium. Guys had worked hard to save money, buy their tickets, and get off work. Now everything else would have to wait. Bills wouldn't get paid. Lawns wouldn't be mowed. Kid's soccer games would have to go on without dad. Wives would have to make it this weekend without their husbands. Something big was happening.

The smell of hot dogs, churros, and popcorn only added to the anticipation in the air. Men were cheering, chatting, and chewing.

Was it a big football game between college rivals? Was it the NFL play-offs? No and no.

We were in the Los Angeles Coliseum, but no uniformed teams were down on the field. Instead, speakers were about to stir men to action at a Promise Keepers conference. Promise Keepers is a national organization committed to developing Christian men of integrity. Through large events and small groups, men are encouraged to be accountable to each other and keep their promises to God, their wives, and to each other.

We were attending Promise Keepers Los Angeles, 1996. The men were comfortable in the stadium setting; most guys were used to sitting next to 75,000 sweating fans. The theme of the Promise Keepers conference was "Break Down the Walls." The emphasis was on reconciliation. Speakers would exhort men to break down the walls that usually separate us: walls of racial, ethnic, and denominational differences.

Soon speaker after speaker challenged us not to pre-judge each other or be competitive. But before the con-ference got underway, I noticed something about us guys.

You can put a male in a stadium, take away the game, and he'll still act like a guy. Which means, of course, he'll act like he is still at a football game. Now I'm not saying that the men should have adopted fake British accents, crossed their legs, and sipped on tea. But I am saying, "Guys will be guys."

In the Coliseum, men quickly adapted to their envi-ronment. They began shouting, running, strutting, and checking each other out. There was so much testos-terone in the place that men were bound to act like roost-ers on parade. I'm not making a value judgment here, just an observation.

I was in the Coliseum for about two minutes before a huge Styrofoam airplane glider almost nailed me. This thing soared from the upper deck. It had a four-foot wingspan. Thousands of men were cheering as the head-bombing aircraft glided downward, clipping the ears of the unaware. It became like the Coliseum of ancient Rome: innocent Christians being attacked for the diver-sion and pleasure of others. I thought it was amusing at first, but then I noticed the intensity of the men on the upper deck. They were taking this *very* seriously.

Were these unemployed aircraft engineers who were doing some testing like they used to at work? Were they disgruntled postal workers lashing out at the general public for putting the stamps upside down? What moti-vated these men to be so competitive about their toy planes?

Six or seven of these monstrous toys were gliding around the stadium. They would be carried back up to the upper decks and astronaut-pitchers would hurl them over the railing into space. If the "pilot" made a good pitch, he would thrust his fist into the air and grunt. It must be some primal scream only heard in the rain forest of Brazil and the laboratories at Hughes Aircraft.

A LITTLE EXPERIMENT

As I munched on my Colossal Dog (with the only thing "colossal" about it being the price—about 78 cents per bite), I decided to do a little sociological research. The subject? male competitiveness. Why were these guys so competitive?

I began with a thesis: Put a civil, soft-spoken male in an athletic, testosterone-laden environment, and he'll start acting (and possibly walking) like Sylvester Stallone. The reason is a guy's competitive nature, and this setting heightened that nature.

Remember, the purpose of the conference was to help men mature and grow. By the behavior I was observing, there was a genuine need for this kind of conference. But it's not the men's fault. It was the environment, I thought.

Thus, my sociological experiment: I'd watch and see if the environment made the man. I observed a young man of about twenty years launch his giant glider over the rail. As he lunged forward, his foot slipped and he almost toppled over the railing. But he caught himself and saved his life. The glider soared down until it caught an updraft. It circled higher and higher, then slowly; it began a cascading spiral to the field. The crowd was ecstatic. The young man drove his arms into the air, grunted, and pounded his chest.

As I observed his behavior, one thought came to mind, *Maybe Darwin was right after all.*

I am sure this young man came to the Coliseum thinking about the stimulating speakers he was about to hear or the inspiring worship he would participate in; but something happened when he walked through the tunnel and into the machismo atmosphere. The warrior took over! He was not alone. And the more I looked, the more I saw my thesis being lived out in the crowd setting: men, surrounded by other men, want to compete.

Guys were seeing how far they could throw a football from the top of the stadium. Frisbees soared through the air, dodging bouncing beach balls. I even noticed a few of those windup, rubber-band-propelled gliders with the cheap red plastic props. Remember those?

Guys were being guys. They had brought their toys. They were doing what guys do when they don't have anything else they should be doing—they compete.

THE COMPETITION REFLEX

What is it about this competition reflex? It is as natural for boys as it is for men.

Take two boys and sit them on a log. Tell them to stay there. In thirty seconds they will be having a rock-throwing contest.

"I bet you can't hit that tree!"

"Oh yes I can, watch."

"I can throw farther than you."

"No you can't."

"See, I told you."

"I bet you can't hit that squirrel."

"Can too!"

This is how hunting began in prehistoric times.

Guys are competitive. Since we don't fight tribe to tribe anymore, we have chosen new tribes; we call them "My Team." Sometimes a guy's commitment to his team and his passion for it may create problems at home.

VOLLEYBALL WARRIOR WILL

Guys are inherently competitive. I remember our meek and mild youth pastor. He was short, thin and scholarly—but put him on a volleyball court and he went nuts!

Wimpy Will (as we affectionately called him) became Warrior Will. Jumping, screaming, pointing, taunting, and challenging became his style of play. Was this the same powder puff who drove a lime green Pinto and spent his free time studying Greek? (We also called him "Greek Geek.") The volleyball court did something to Will. It changed his personality. He went from meek and mild to downright wild. He hated to lose and usually blamed one of us kids. I'll never forget a time his team lost. Will threw the ball out of the court and stomped off pouting.

"Some Christian leader," sarcastically quipped one of the guys.

We didn't have much respect for him. He knew Scripture. He could play his guitar well. But his fierce competitiveness disqualified him from being taken seriously. Out-of-control competitiveness can make a fool of any man.

A SOFTBALL SAGA

Take for instance the time-honored tradition of church softball teams.

Because it's softball and because the teams are from churches, you can expect civil and fair play fostered by a spirit of camaraderie. If you believe that, I'd like to sell you some land in Florida.

There are few sports more vicious than men's church softball. Men's church softball makes hockey look like a church picnic. It makes running with the bulls in Spain look like a kindergarten class walking to the playground, each holding the rope. Get my point?

I'll never forget that summer I played on the team. We had won more games than we had lost. We were getting ready to play the Lutherans. These guys were tough. I guess it was the spirit of Martin Luther pulsing in their veins. They had something to prove. They had already knocked off the Catholics (like true reformers). They pummeled the Presbyterians. They mangled the Methodists. They had embarrassed the Episcopalians. Now they were going to try to bash the Baptists. They pulled up to the field in large vans. They jumped out at once. They looked different from us. They had matching uniforms—bright white uniforms with pinstripes. And we had our uniforms—matching tee shirts and whatever cap we could find. They looked like the Yankees. We looked like nerds.

But softball is not how you look but how you play. And that's what worried me. Our play could be summed up in a word: unpredictable. Sometimes we could hit the ball, sometimes we couldn't. Some games we had an awesome defense, and other games we made a dozen errors. The Lutherans weren't sure whom they were dealing with. But they didn't look scared.

As they did team warm-ups and shouted their push-up count, "49,50, 51. . . ," we began to get worried. We never did push-ups. Let alone count them out loud and in unison! It was frightening.

The game got underway and we did OK. At least until we had to take the field. They would score eight runs before we finally came to bat. Then our leadoff guy got to first on an error; now it was my turn.

The pressure was on. My team needed me to advance the lead runner and get on first. I knew what I needed to do: *Hit the ball.*

After two quick strikes, I knew I had to take the third pitch. I couldn't risk getting struck out. I couldn't live with the teasing and the shame. My teammates were shouting, "C'mon, batter." The Lutherans were shouting, "C'mon, batter." Children in the bleachers shouted, "C'mon, batter."

I felt the pressure; I just had to swing. The pitcher released the ball; it seemed to come to me in slow motion. I concentrated on the ball and blocked out the cheers and jeers. As the ball neared home plate it began a wicked drop. If I were going to connect, I would have to step for-

ward and hit the ball low. I leaned forward and stretched
my back; I took a step as I unwound the bat.

"Cracckk!" went the bat against the ball. Well, not really; that was just my imagination. What actually happened probably sounded more like "crick."

But I actually hit the softball. I almost fell down, too,
because I had to reach way out in front of me to make
contact with the ball.

But I did hit it. The ball flew (as opposed to dribbled)
past the pitcher and deep into the infield, almost to second base. I scurried to first base, but I got thrown out.

As I walked back to my bench, in total humiliation, I
noticed the Lutherans on their bench. They sat smirking.
I even saw one sipping on a beer.

*What are they doing drinking beer at a church softball
game?* I asked myself. *What do they think this is, base-
ball?*

I was irritated not only at how poorly I played, but at
the cavalier attitude demonstrated by the other team.
They seemed to be out here just to have fun.

It bugged me. Didn't they know this was Church Wars?

My zeal for denominational turf consumed me. The
guy drinking beer started to bug me. "There must be
some kind of rule against that! I mean after all, this is a
church league." I continued to fuss and whine about it.

I figured, *If we can't beat them on the field, let's beat
them with a technicality off the field.* It's pitiful, it's pointless, but it's true. A competitive spirit can make fools of
us all.

In my self-righteousness, I hadn't noticed that my
whining was more offensive and potentially dangerous
than the guy sipping a Bud. So I began to complain
aloud. My mouth got me in trouble.

One of the larger Lutherans came over and asked me
what I was griping about.

"You guys aren't following the rules!" I complained.

"What rules are you talking about?" the big guy asked.

"The rules about beer at the game. You are not supposed to bring it."

"Says who? This is private property. It's not a park. He's breaking no law."

"There are rules about alcohol."

"Show me in the rule book." The big guy manufactured one out of his back pocket.

"It's here somewhere." I flipped through the book in quiet desperation. I found nothing.

"What did I tell you?" asked the pinstriped giant.

"Well, there should be a rule."

"But there isn't! Can we get back to playing?"

I felt even smaller. I had judged these guys to be immature impostors, but in reality, I was the fake.

AN UNHEALTHY COMPETITIVE SPIRIT

Double standards. Legalistic rules. Trying to look good in front of others. All of these can be symptoms of a competitive spirit. Healthy competition and sportsmanship are one thing, but a competitive spirit can be dangerous. A competitive spirit competes off the field. It competes from the dugout and outside the clubhouse.

When a guy moves from liking competition to developing a competitive spirit, he begins to push too hard. He goes over the line. He doesn't know when to let things go. He has the compulsion to win at all costs.

I am not talking about healthy competition; I'm talking about unhealthy competition. The kind that eats at you and makes you lose control. It is the kind of rage that makes you do foolish things. It leads to angry outbursts, hostility, and division. These aren't pleasing to God.

I lost my perspective in that softball game. I forgot what was really important. I was focused on how my team and I looked. I was more concerned about winning a game than winning people for Christ. I had lost sight of the big picture.

We tend to be more competitive when we think it's about us. Our egos get in the way of handling the competitive pressure. In sports there will always be competition. When does it become a problem? When our competitive spirit causes us to lose control and say things or do things which are over the line.

Healthy competition is giving your all on the court or playing field, but playing within the rules. It's challenging your opponent without being rude or condescending. It's trying to get the edge without going over the line. A healthy competitor pushes himself to go beyond what he might normally exert, but is still in control. In control of his mouth, his hands, his feet, and most of all, his attitude.

We don't always see this in professional sports. For example, several National Basketball Association players have been suspended and fined for pushing referees, physically attacking their coaches, and general mayhem on the court. What is going on with these NBA stars?

I think they have lost sight of the big picture. Somehow they confused the sport of basketball with a showcase for their arrogance. They don't like being told no. They have allowed their pride to infiltrate their sense of competition. The result? A win-at-any-cost attitude. Even if it means physically intimidating officials.

What can we learn from the NBA "bad boys"?

There will always be an authority we will need to submit to. Even with all-star skills and a multimillion dollar income, all men need to be under authority. We can maintain a healthy sense of competition if we remember we are men under authority. For basketball players, it is the NBA official. For Christian men, we need to submit to the Ultimate Official. God never makes a questionable call. He sees them all clearly.

When we remember that we give an account to the Righteous Referee, it can temper our competitive spirit.

As followers of God, we need to be the kind of men who can submit to authority (see Romans 13:1–2). It doesn't always have to be "my way or the highway." A man who hasn't come to terms with authority will be tempted to challenge it. He may allow his competitive spirit to influence him to act or say things that are out of bounds.

I am not saying Christian men need to be wimps. I am saying we need to have a healthy sense of competition, which means we try our best to win. But we play fair. We don't take shortcuts. We don't undermine the authority of the official. We compete in such a way that it demonstrates our best effort.

The apostle Paul summarized well the proper attitudes toward competition, submission, and self-control:

> Do you not know that in a race all the runners run, but only one gets the prize? Run in such a way as to get the prize. Everyone who competes in the games goes into strict training. They do it to get a crown that will not last; but we do it to get a crown that will last forever. Therefore I do not run like a man running aimlessly; I do not fight like a man beating the air. No, I beat my body and make it my slave so that after I have preached to others, I myself will not be disqualified for the prize. (1 Corinthians 9:24–27)

Let's run to win!

Guidelines for Real Guys

Principle 7: A real guy competes fairly and displays self-control, because he has learned to submit to authority.

8
Relationships (and Other Girl Stuff)

*M*en have one extra chromosome," explained Tim Taylor on TV's *Home Improvement,* "the Y chromosome."

"So?" replied Jill.

"So men are always asking *why* do we always have to talk about relationships?!"

Men aren't always more analytical than women, but they often are. It's another way men differ from women. Remember menism number two: Guys aren't too concerned about commitment in their relationships. They have grown up thinking relationships are "girl stuff."

A guy's sense of self is defined through his achievement and acquisition: "You are what you do." Guys value achievement, power, competency, and efficiency. They are always looking for ways to prove themselves and develop their strength and skills. Guys are on the hunt for results.

Women are different (you probably noticed). Women are in pursuit of relationships, not results. They aren't as interested in accomplishments, things, and power. Women are more interested in relationships, feelings, and communication. A woman's sense of self is defined through her feelings and the strength of her relationships.

Since guys are hunting for results and women are looking for relationships, it can lead to problems. Consider Dave Barry's insight:

Women have a lot of trouble accepting [men's little interest in developing relationships.] Despite millions of years of overwhelming evidence to the contrary, women are convinced that guys must spend a certain amount of time thinking about the relationship. How could they not? How could a guy see another human being day after day, night after night, sharing countless hours with this person, becoming physically intimate—how can a guy be doing these things and not be thinking about their relationship? This is what women figure. They are wrong.[1]

Suzanne (my wife) and I went out on a date. I actually asked her out and took a shower and everything. We went to see a Mel Gibson movie. I knew it would put her in a good mood. It worked! After staring at Mel's big baby blues for two hours, she was in a chummy, romantic mood. Which, if you are an astute observer of females, means she was talking a lot. She was feeling loved, valued, and close to me. As we drove home, she shared intimately:

"I just think it is so wonderful that . . ."

I really didn't catch what she was saying, but her tone of voice was warm. Then I noticed something: so was the engine temperature gauge! As she chatted on and on about people, relationships, and who knows what; I fixed my eyes on the dash gauge. *The car is running hot! I just had it serviced. I wonder what is wrong?*

"Feelings . . . friendships . . ." She was saying something, and I was sort of hearing it: "Growing as a person . . . blah . . . blah."

I admit it; I tuned her out. I had more important things to work on, I figured. *Why is the car running ten degrees hotter than usual?* I was on a mission. I needed a solution. Suzanne talked until we got home. Of course I responded as a sensitive and caring guy: "Uh-huh . . . sure . . . yup."

I had no clue what she was talking about. And to make it worse, I didn't know why the car was running so hot—still don't. How could I focus on relationship? I needed *results!*

Guys want results. Women want relationship. Guys want solutions. Women want to share. It's a course headed for conflict. Fortunately, I have some good news, although it is again from Dave Barry:

> Contrary to what many women believe, it's fairly easy to develop a long-term, stable and intimate, mutually fulfilling relationship with a guy. Of course, this guy has to be a Labrador retriever. With human guys, it's extremely difficult. This is because guys don't really grasp what women mean by the term *relationship.*[2]

DEFINING "RELATIONSHIP"

So men, let's start by being sure we understand the word. *Relationship* implies a connection between two participants. A relationship means belonging and bonding to each other. This is just the opposite of most guys' natural drive. As hunters and gatherers we like to hit the trail. We like the idea of being free to hunt. We don't want to get "pinned down" in the teepee having tea and trapped in some "dumb conversation." Guys have a built-in tendency to pull away. Women have a built-in tendency to attach. They like sitting in the teepee, sipping tea, and chatting. They are connecting.

This isn't just my male opinion. Carol Gilligan, professor of education at Harvard University, contrasted the differences in her pivotal book *In a Different Voice:*

> Relationships, and particularly issues of dependency, are experienced differently by women and men. For boys and men, separation and individuation [a fancy word for becoming individuals] are critically tied to gender identity since separation from the mother is essential for the development of masculinity. For girls and women, issues of femininity or feminine identity do not depend on the achievement of separation from the mother or on the progress of individuation.

Since masculinity is defined through separation while femi-
ninity is defined through attachment, male gender identity is
threatened by intimacy while female gender identity is
threatened by separation. Thus males tend to have difficulty
with relationships, while females tend to have problems with
individuation.[3]

In other words, guys are pushing away, and women
are seeking to connect. Guys feel trapped with trying to
avoid relationships but sensing they need them. This can
be confusing; on his journey toward becoming a free
agent, he becomes aware of his need to connect. It can
be a very conflicting experience. To bring order to relationships, some guys develop rules. They are anxious to
control what they fear—intimacy. Guys, in their desire to
control, may seek to manage relationships. They sense
the power and potential of relationships, and they don't
want to be under their influence. They don't want to become a victim of a relationship.

This may seem strange, yet that's how we guys respond. We know we are designed to be in relationship,
but we aren't sure what that is supposed to look like, and
it makes us nervous. So we seek to control our relationships by keeping them at arms' length. It's true of most
guys' relationships with women *and* men. We really don't
feel that confident about relationships. In fact, we intentionally limit relationships.

In the "modern" world, many of us are not willing to commit
to the time required to share more and more of ourselves
with more and more people. We start by limiting the number
of our friendships. Then we limit the level of our openness.
Sure enough, we create more time to do other things, but we
sacrifice a lot as well. Perhaps the problem is really selfishness. Yet self-enhancement occurs when the virtues of friends
rub off on us.[4]

I feel like I am a better person after being around
good friends. I feel more alive. More valuable. More sig-

nificant. Relationships add to our lives, but they do take work. For guys, relationship building doesn't come naturally. The irony is that the same skills that guys use at work to build relationships often get left at the office. When they come home, they falsely assume that their relationship with their wife won't take the same initiative and follow-through as work relationships.

I told her I loved her at the wedding. She should know that. If I change my mind, I'll let her know, they reason.

"For a man to enjoy a good relationship with a woman, he must adjust his expectations," writes Gray. "Instead of thinking his work is over when he comes home, he must realize that *having a relationship is also part of his work.* ... Too often men assume that once they are married, the work of having a relationship is over. Realistically, that is when it begins" [italics added].[5]

Gray may be a best-selling author and counselor, but the concept of devotion and committed work in marriage originated in the Scriptures:

> Husbands, love your wives, just as Christ loved the church and gave himself up for her to make her holy, cleansing her by the washing with water through the word, and to present her to himself as a radiant church, without stain or wrinkle or any other blemish, but holy and blameless. In this same way, husbands ought to love their wives as their own bodies. He who loves his wife loves himself. After all, no one ever hated his own body, but he feeds and cares for it, just as Christ does the church. (Ephesians 5:25–29)

Guys, if you are married, let me ask you, "Is your wife radiant?" Does she beam with brilliance due to all the care you give her (kind of like your favorite car did)? Does she radiate your efforts to help her become all she can be? What have you given up for her? Does she sense that she is the top priority in your life?

I have met wives who have radiated this kind of

Christlike love and care from their husbands. They emanate a beauty and a confidence that can't be purchased. Relationships take work; especially male-female relationships. I know of guys who take really good care of their bodies: they exercise at the gym four days a week; they eat healthy, manage stress, get plenty of rest, and avoid tobacco and alcohol. They know how to love their own bodies, but they don't know how to love their wives. They have falsely assumed that their wives don't need nurture or investment. They are on the road to divorce.

What do women need from us? Gray has found seven key ways women feel loved: (1) caring; (2) openness; (3) understanding; (4) respect; (5) acceptance; (6) grace (allowing for growth; expecting process, not perfection); and (7) encouragement.[6]

Significantly; the first letter of each word forms an acrostic: COURAGE. It takes courage to have a relationship with a woman. Some men have backed away from a promising relationship with their wives because they didn't have this kind of courage.

Courage to show her that you care.

Courage to be open and vulnerable.

Courage to seek first to understand, rather than be understood.

Courage to demonstrate respect.

Courage to accept her as she is.

Courage to grant her grace and expect growth over time, not perfection.

Courage to pour courage into her, to support her, and to try new things. To be on her side.

Guys, this is your checklist to see if you are loving your wife like Christ loved His bride, the church. It's costly. It will take effort. But it's the right way to work on a relationship.

CAN GUYS BE FRIENDS?

A guy never wants to hear from another guy: "Let's talk about our relationship."

It doesn't seem right. That is something we expect from a woman, but certainly *not* from another guy. But if we never talk about our relationships, will they ever improve? And guys need relationships with other guys, not just with women.

Jeff, a firefighter in his late thirties, came to talk with me about his male friendships, or rather, his lack of them.

"I feel like I don't have any close friends," he said with regret.

"Have you ever talked with potential friends and let them know you would like to get to know them better; maybe do something together you both enjoy?"

"No," he looked down at his shoes; "I have never done that."

"Are you happy with your current results?"

"No, of course not. That's why I'm talking to you."

"If you aren't happy with the results, then you need to change your current approach."

"What do you mean?"

"That you will risk relationship and potential rejection for the possible payoff of a friendship."

"I need to learn how to be a friend."

"Exactly."

"Where do I start?" he asked sincerely.

"Realize that God designed us for relationship. He even said, 'It is not good for the man to be alone' [Genesis 2:18]. This was the first time God called something 'not good.' Isolation is not good; it is not part of God's plan. We can't experience the abundant life as Lone Rangers. Even God Himself is three persons. The Trinity illustrates God's desire for relationship and community."

"You mean I can't grow to be a mature Christian man by myself."

"I don't think so. Everywhere I look in Scripture I see guys connecting one-on-one or in small groups. Even Jesus sent out His advance teams in twos."

"Where did I come up with this strong-man-does-it-alone idea?"

"From our culture; it's not from the Bible. Scripture affirms individuality only as it contributes to community."

"You mean each person has something to contribute?"

"Right. And if you aren't connected to a group of men, they miss out as well as you. Being connected with a band of men is Christ's model."

Jeff wondered aloud why he seemed unable to connect, so I suggested it was because of feelings of shame.

"What do you mean?" he asked.

"Guys don't open up with other guys because they are embarrassed," I explained. "Embarrassed of their sins, of their failures, or of their spiritual immaturity. Shame keeps guys silent. It is a destroyer of men. Shame brings isolation. Shame makes pretenders of us all; it keeps us from being authentic with each other."

"What is the remedy? I mean, I really can see myself distancing from other men because of things I am not proud of. So, what do I do?"

"The answer is not a remedy, it's a relationship," I answered. "You need to recognize that you are God's son. See your identity as a beloved son. Take your sins—your mistakes, your hidden habits, and your pride—and unload them at the Cross. Jesus died for those burdens. Trade in your shame for sonship."

"If we see ourselves as sons, does it help us relate to each other?"

"Yeah. It helps us not posture and perform for each other. Since we are sons by what Christ did for us, we don't have to show off or pretend. After all, we are brothers—we don't have to impress each other. Instead, we can spend time being authentic and getting to know each other. The relationship is different because it is secure; it is not based on achievement or any other conditions. Because of God's unconditional love for us, we can be free to relate to each other."

"That is what I need."

"Just remember who you are and who your Father is."

It's true for any man: When we remember that we are valued sons loved by a heavenly Father, we are free to draw close to other needy men in healthy relationships.

We need authentic and strong relationships with other guys—the kind that make us better men. Proverbs instructs us, "As iron sharpens iron, so one man sharpens another" (27:17).

If we are going to be the sharp and prepared tools that God wants us to be—at home, at work, and in the community—we need to have an iron-sharpens-iron experience with another guy or a small group of guys. Sure there will be some sparks. There will be some heat. Count on some resistance. But without the contact, and the chiseling effect of truth, we will remain dull and distant.

OUR FEAR OF FRIENDSHIPS

Sounds good, you may think, *but it isn't easy to get involved in new relationships. And it's risky. It seems safer and easier to pretend I'm better off alone.*

That's an honest reaction. Sometimes, when we hear the word *friend,* it frightens us. It brings to mind obligations, commitments, and being vulnerable. Another reason we fear male friendships is the distorted influence of our culture that implies if two men are close, they are probably gay. We don't want to be branded homosexual; so we keep each other at arm's length. But true friendship doesn't have to be a burden; it doesn't have to be possessive or sexual. "The love of friendship rejoices in the freedom of the friend, and thus lets the friend go continually to grow and become all that the friend was meant to be."[7]

A third reason we don't develop relationships with other guys is the time and work it requires. That's true;

friendships are far more demanding than acquaintances. But the dividends for investing your time are many, including honesty, commitment, and camaraderie. As counselor James Osterhaus notes:

> The people involved [in friendships] experience an ever-deepening bond as they slowly learn to open their lives to each other. This relationship involves an honesty and commitment that allows each to challenge the other to ever-greater degrees of openness. Most men look upon acquaintances as friends because they are not able to build beyond the casual camaraderie that men develop at places of work or leisure. Little effort is put into these relationships, and they can terminate as quickly as they begin. Having true friends requires being able to reach out to other people, to engage those people, establish a relationship, and maintain that relationship over time.[8]

WHAT IT TAKES

Let's assume you see the value of having relationships with another guy (or guys). What is required for guys to have a friendship? I believe there are at least five essential elements for guys to develop an iron-sharpens-iron relationship with each other: (1) a desire to connect, (2) feeling secure with yourself, (3) willing to have fun, (4) a desire for authenticity, and (5) being comfortable with emotions. Do you have the following five desires and attitudes?

- *The desire to connect.* A guy must be willing to leave the cultural myth of the independent macho stud in order to discover the value of a friendship with another guy. In our culture, we like the idea of the rugged individual more than the value of community. Autonomy has become the symbol of power, virility, and freedom. When a man faces pressure, he tends to withdraw. Yet men need to connect with others. When a man is ready to give up the illusion that he can do it alone, he is on his way to developing friendships with other men.

- *Personal security.* It is risky developing a relationship with another guy; he might reject you; you may not feel comfortable with the vulnerability; and you may discover something you don't like, or worse, he might. It takes a guy who is willing to deal with his fears and the risks of friendship. It also takes someone who is relatively secure in what he believes. He must be confident about his critical core beliefs and flexible about the nonessentials. In other words, he needs to know when to fight and when to walk away. Not everything is a battleground; a secure man knows this. There will be disagreement among friends. If you have personal security and confidence, you can agree to disagree when you have disagreements. Differing points of view do not have to terminate a relationship. In fact, they often strengthen them.

- *Enjoying fun together.* It could be a joke over breakfast, an amusing anecdote in the small group, or a day enjoying a mutual interest; but guys need to laugh together if they are going to develop a relationship. Laughter and fun bonds guys together. Fun creates a shared experience. If guys are going to develop a relationship of depth and meaning, they will need to log some fun times together. At first glance, this appears to be a paradox; but the reality is, guys won't put the work into a relationship they don't enjoy.

- *Authenticity.* Guys are often insecure and afraid, so they project strength and bravado. The strategy works if the goal is image control, but it keeps men from being real with each other. Deep inside, most guys are looking for a place where they are known and can be themselves. They are desperate for relationships where they can be real and are still ac-

cepted. Honesty is critical for all relationships. It is
allowing truth to be at the core of our friendship.
Being authentic means allowing others to see the
real you, strengths and weaknesses.

- *Comfortable with emotions.* Yes, as we noted in
chapter 8, emotions are for men as well as women.
We have emotions; we might as well get used to
them. In fact, we might want to try to understand
them and become comfortable with them because
they aren't going away! If two guys are going to try
and develop a friendship, some emotions are bound
to show up. They could be positive (enjoyment) or
negative (anger); but there will be emotions that
emerge as a result of your budding friendship.
Emotions are normal responses we make to the environment around us. We should expect them in
our relationships with other guys.

A final word about emotions. Guys will often try to
deny their emotions or dictate their emotions, seeking to
control them. May I suggest a third approach? Try dis-
cussing them. Talking about our emotions with other
guys helps us understand ourselves, understand each
other, and grow closer by increasing trust. That's another
good reason for a relationship: to understand who we are
as we acknowledge our feelings to others.

I am not sure we can understand life and ourselves
unless we have a few close and trusted friends who aren't
afraid to ask the hard questions. We need to be accountable if we expect to grow. As Solomon wrote, "The pur-
poses of a man's heart are deep waters, but a man of
understanding draws them out" (Proverbs 20:5).

Can guys be friends? Of course, but for most of us it
doesn't come easily. But if you are like me, you really
long for a friend who understands your heart and helps
you sort through the deep waters.

How can you get a friend who is a man of understanding? Become one.

Guidelines for Real Guys

Principle 8: A real guy knows he needs close relationships with other guys if he is to grow as a man.

9
The Blame Game, Pride, and Other Unmanly Acts

I once saw a book entitled *We've Been Through a Lot Together—And Most of It Was Your Fault.* As guys we often feel that way. When the going gets tough, we want to blame someone else. If failure occurs, we are quick to point to a "fall guy" (or girl). Blame comes easy to guys; it must be built into our genes.

Our tendency to be quick to blame really makes women mad. Of course, we have been blaming women since the Garden of Eden. Women have a right to be mad.

Consider the biblical record:

> Then the man and his wife heard the sound of the Lord God as he was walking in the garden in the cool of the day, and they hid from the Lord God among the trees of the garden. But the Lord God called to the man, "Where are you?"
>
> He answered, "I heard you in the garden, and I was afraid because I was naked; so I hid."
>
> And he said, "Who told you that you were naked? Have you eaten from the tree that I commanded you not to eat from?"
>
> The man said, "The woman you put here with me—she gave me some fruit from the tree, and I ate it."
>
> Then the Lord God said to the woman, "What is this you have done?"
>
> The woman said, "The serpent deceived me, and I ate."
> (Genesis 3:8–13)

SHAME AND BLAME

You could call this story, "Shame and Blame." Adam was instantly aware of his nakedness when he broke God's law and ate of the fruit. Broken rules lead to shame. Shame leads to broken relationship. Adam tried to hide from God.

Consider how ridiculous the scene was. Adam had observed God make all kinds of animals and parade them in front of him for naming. He knew God was the Creator. God made the trees and the plants, including the leaves Adam used to try to hide his nakedness. Yet, somehow Adam forgot this after he sinned by eating the fruit. He forgot God made everything and knew everything.

Sin will do that to you. It makes you forget the really important stuff and focus on the ridiculous. Adam's sin caused his loss of innocence. He now experienced a strange, new emotion: shame. When we disobey God's rules, shame results, causing us to hide—from each other and from God. Ever since this incident, humans have been hiding from each other and from God.

Shame and blame continues with the second part of the saga—the blame part. When the going gets tough, Adam wimps out. When God asks him, "Have you eaten the fruit I told you not to?" Adam takes the line of least resistance (and backbone). He pins it on his wife.

"The woman you put here with me—she gave me some fruit."

I can imagine him adding, "It wasn't my idea. I even told her we shouldn't, but she was so convincing. If you didn't want me to give in, you shouldn't have made her so beautiful and manipulative."

Eve quickly learns the blame game—she pins it on the serpent.

Snakes have had a bad rap ever since.

In a few short minutes, a woman and a man learned a bad habit that they have passed on to their descendants: avoiding personal responsibility by blaming.

Why is this such a big deal? Can't we let blaming slip by as a peculiarity?

No, we can't. Blaming is costly. It is a defense mechanism designed to throw up a smoke screen for personal responsibility. When we blame, we are seeking to avoid accountability for our behavior.

I recently saw a dramatic illustration of blaming. On my way to work I had stopped my car at a four-way stop. I was behind a guy in a Porsche Carrera, and together we watched a scary scene: a woman driving a new Suburban entered from the cross street, began a left turn, and promptly struck a Saturn driven by a teenage girl. The young girl had no time to react. Her Saturn careened off the Suburban and screeched toward the Porsche and me. Right before it slammed into us, it swerved away and crashed into a utility pole.

The Porsche guy and I jumped out and ran to the victims. The girl was injured. The air bag saved her from smashing into the windshield. She was scared, bloody, and pinned in her car. Porsche Guy ran back to his car and called 911 on his cell phone. Suburban Mom was wandering the street in shock. I asked her to sit in her car and try to calm down. I ran back over to talk to Gina, the girl in the Saturn.

"I didn't see her," she cried, tears mingling with blood. "Why did she turn in front of me?"

I ran back to my truck to get some first-aid supplies. The traffic had started to back up. A few came to help, including a huge surfer who hopped out of his truck with a blanket. Surfer and I decided to move our trucks to make room for the paramedics and fire trucks that would soon be there. That's when we encountered the Blame Guy, who was as selfish as he was accusing.

A portly balding man in an old, gray Oldsmobile was honking his horn. He poked his red face out of his window and shouted, "Move your blankity blank cars! You guys are blocking the street!"

The wreckage blocked most of the road. Our cars were in the way because we were the first on the scene, and we were busy attending the injured. But Blame Guy wanted us to move; we were responsible for slowing his plans. He seemed to be retirement age; he certainly wasn't dressed for work. He looked like he was dressed for the golf driving range, located directly down the street.

"Hang on, can't you see there is an accident!" I yelled back at him.

"Yeah, we are helping someone who is hurt. You can wait!" exclaimed Surfer.

But Blame Guy kept honking. It was amazing. He started to merge his huge car into a space behind the wreck. It wouldn't fit, so he tried another angle. He was being totally selfish. We began to move our trucks.

"You guys are causing a huge traffic jam, move your cars!" he shouted out his window as we started our engines.

The surfer had heard enough. He jumped out of his 4x4 and went back to talk to the guy in the Oldsmobile. The man quickly rolled up his window. Surfer pounded on it and said, "Shut up, you selfish jerk! Don't be so impatient. One more word or honk from you and I am going to *pound you!*"

I still can't believe that this little, old man was giving this Hercules lip. Surfer was about 6 feet 4 inches and 240 pounds of taut muscle. People cheered for his response to Blame Guy.

What made this twerp blame us for having to wait a few minutes? I'm still amazed by his behavior. I mean, this is L. A.; mouthing off like he did could have gotten him shot! He obviously had a quick reaction of blaming —even in the midst of a tragedy.

As Surfer and I pulled our trucks out of the way, the Blame Guy screeched by. People shook their heads as he drove by; a few, much more angry by his impatience and blaming, flashed him obscene gestures.

A FOOLISH GAME, THIS BLAME

Blame Guy may be extreme, but he's like most guys who aren't dealing with their own wounds; they tend to blame others. Those who blame are only hiding from themselves and others. They know they are incomplete and wounded, but they don't admit it. Their denial only fuels their shame. They go through the day with a mental tape playing, *You are missing out. You aren't whole.* This causes them to develop a reactive approach to life. They learn to react with blame. They reason, *I'm incomplete, upset, hurt, not respected . . .and it's your fault!*

This reactive style of relating leads to alienation.

I saw it happen in that intersection. The old guy in the Oldsmobile reacted to the situation before he could even think. There were at least thirty people who witnessed his pathetic behavior. He managed to prove himself a self-centered fool in front of an audience.

Blame makes fools of us all. Solomon wrote, "Like a madman shooting firebrands or deadly arrows is a man who deceives his neighbor and says, 'I was only joking!'" (Proverbs 26:18–19).

A pattern of blaming is just an attempt to excuse ourselves from personal accountability. When we blame others, it is an indicator of our self-deception. Deception always leads to bondage. The more we blame, the more we ensnare ourselves. We also deceive ourselves in pretending our behavior (and blaming) doesn't wound those we blame.

Jesus offers freedom. He claimed to be truth and proclaimed, "You will know the truth, and the truth will set you free" (John 8:32).

We can take our wounds to Jesus. We can take our fears to Jesus. We can take our sins to Jesus. And we can say to Him, "These are mine. They belong to me. They belong to no one else. I release them to You."

Guys who blame are holding out. They are foolishly hiding from the One who can help them. Like Adam, we

think a flimsy leaf bikini will hide our nakedness. We use
blame as a covering for our nakedness. Instead, we need
to drop our shame at the Cross. Jesus died for the very
things we are trying to hide. Jesus already paid the price
for our sin and the way it taints who we are.
Your sin is already paid for. Let it go.

PRIDE

Not all guys practice the blame game, of course;
there are other ways we act unmanly in our actions. We
will look at just a few. Besides blame, pride is one option
we guys frequently use. Pride comes so easy. We don't
have to work at acquiring pride. We don't need to attend
classes like "Arrogance 101" or "Ego Enhancement
Skills." We pick it up on our own. Patrick Morley has
written about pride's appeal to men:

> Pride is a sin of comparison in which we compare our
> strengths to the other fellow's weaknesses. In order to make
> ourselves feel better we put other people down, sometimes
> verbally and sometimes just mentally. The easiest way to look
> down on others is to pick out people of less stature and ac-
> complishment. And it's particularly easy to pick out other
> people's weaknesses to compare to our strengths.
> The subtle sin of pride beguiles every Christian man. The
> most invisible of sins, pride seeps into the Christian life like
> water oozes into the moat around a sandcastle on the beach.
> It requires no effort on our part to get, but all of our strength
> to keep out.[1]

Pride is the enemy of true Christlike character. As the
apostle James wrote, "God opposes the proud but gives
grace to the humble" (James 4:6).
Pride is subtle, yet powerful. Before you know it, it
has control. Pride is dangerous in itself, but it can also
lead to a variety of other problems and sins. According to
Proverbs 6:16–19, "There are six things the Lord hates,
seven that are detestable to him: haughty eyes, a lying

tongue, hands that shed innocent blood, a heart that devises wicked schemes, feet that are quick to rush into evil, a false witness who pours out lies and a man who stirs up dissension among brothers."

These are some of the strongest words in Scripture. God hates pride. It makes Him nauseous. Like rotten food, pride is detestable. Notice that the first item God hates is "haughty eyes." This is the kind of arrogant perspective that looks down on everyone else. To be haughty is to consider yourself superior to others.

Pride is a gateway sin to other sins. Just like we have gateway drugs, such as marijuana, that lead to other drugs, pride is a gateway sin. Next to those "haughty eyes" in verse 17, Solomon listed the following outcomes: lying, violence, wicked scheming, evil behavior, false witness, and conflict ("dissension").

Can you see how pride can open the door to these other sins?

Pride makes us depend on our own strengths. It leaves us to our own perspective and experience. Pride, like blaming, sets us up to be fools. In a futile attempt to cover ourselves, we lie—or we might blame. If the heat keeps up, we might recoil with violence. To protect ourselves we might scheme wicked plans for evil behavior. When pressed to speak the truth, pride will cause us to bear false witness. Pride doesn't lead to peace, it destroys it. Inevitably, pride will cause conflict. It might even start a fight.

Untreated pride can keep us unhealthy.

HERE'S MUD IN YOUR EYES

Our pride can even keep us from God's healing. Remember Naaman, the commander of the army of the king of Aram? His story is told in 2 Kings 5. A great man and a mighty warrior, Naaman received much acclaim for his victories. But there was one foe he couldn't conquer—his leprosy.

His wife's servant, a captured Israelite girl, noticed

his plight. She said to her mistress, "If only my master would see the prophet who is in Samaria! He would cure him of his leprosy" (v. 3).

Naaman told the king about what she had said. The king gave Naaman permission to go to the king of Israel and seek healing. He also gave Naaman gifts to offer the king of Israel and a letter of protection and introduction. Naaman was used to dealing with those who were in charge. Letters and gifts from the king were what he was accustomed to.

The king of Israel, however, didn't know what to do when he received the request. "Why does this fellow send someone to me to be cured of his leprosy?" he asked. He was suspicious of this mighty warrior who was an uneasy ally at times, but usually an enemy of Israel. "See how he is trying to pick a quarrel with me!" (v. 7).

Things were a little tense.

Enter Elisha—man of God. He sent word to the king, "Send Naaman to me. I am the prophet in Israel." I think Naaman really didn't listen to the servant girl. She said see the prophet in Israel, not the king. Being the CEO type, Naaman heard "king." Not being a believer, he probably didn't understand the function of a prophet, which is to be the spiritual leader of a tribe. Naaman was still trying to deal with his leprosy through political or military protocol.

Naaman charged off with his horses and chariots to Elisha's house. Elisha sent out a messenger to the great commander, perched in his chariot.

"Go jump in the Jordan River and dip seven times. Then your leprosy will be healed and your flesh restored" (v. 10, author's paraphrase).

The muddy cesspool they call Jordan River! Naaman recoiled at the thought.

He went away angry and said, "I thought that he would surely come out to me and stand and call on the name of the Lord his God, wave his hand over the spot and cure me of my leprosy. Why couldn't I do this in a clean river back home?" Naaman was offended and in a rage. He wasn't used to people sending messengers. He liked to deal directly with the man in charge. His pride had been hurt. His pride almost cost him his healing.

His servants worked on him, "If the prophet had told you to do some great thing, would you not have done it? How much more, then, when he tells you, 'Wash and be cleansed'!" (v. 13).

Naaman was used to doing "great" things; he wasn't comfortable doing small, humiliating things, like dipping in a muddy river. That was Elisha's point: to experience the mighty hand of God we must first be humble.

Finally, Naaman went down to the river. What were his thoughts as he dipped seven times in the muddy Jordan? Perhaps:

Look at all the people watching me.

Dip.

I wonder if they think I'm nuts.

Dip.

Here is the "valiant warrior, commander in chief!" How embarrassing.

Dip.

They make me deal with this weirdo prophet. The king isn't even here!

Dip.

I wonder if this is a practical joke, or a military trap?

He dipped again.

I wish I were doing this in a clean river back home. I am getting mud in my eyes.

And again.

What was it about that servant girl that made her believe that her God would heal me? Hmm . . .

He dipped once more.

And then Naaman, so preoccupied with himself, stared in amazement at his wet, glistening skin.

"Hey!" he shouted, capturing the attention of everyone on the riverbank. "I am healed. It really worked!"

People cheered. Believers shouted, "Praise God!"

Naaman dried off and went to Elisha's house and declared to the prophet, "Now I know that there is no God in all the world except in Israel" (v. 15).

Naaman's pride almost kept him from God's healing. As guys we like to do great things. We like accomplishments and achievement. We don't like doing small things. We avoid the insignificant in pursuit of the noteworthy. But usually, God's way is the smaller and less noticeable.

God's way is the "still small voice"; it's a baby born in a cattle stall. Jesus chooses lowly fishermen. Rather than sitting in the palace of kings, Jesus has children sit on His lap.

To experience God's blessing, we must first give up the notion that God needs us and our resources. We must come to Him with humility and dependence. We come to Him on our knees.

A real guy acts in humility, resisting blame, pride, and their allies. He heeds James's words:

> Submit yourselves, then, to God. Resist the devil, and he will flee from you. Come near to God and he will come near to you. Wash your hands, you sinners, and purify your hearts, you double-minded. Grieve, mourn and wail. Change your laughter to mourning and your joy to gloom. Humble yourselves before the Lord, and he will lift you up. (James 4:7-10)

Guidelines for Real Guys

Principle 9: A real guy is humble, for he knows humility will keep him from doing foolish things.

10

I Want to Be a Macho Man

*G*uys like places where they can be guys. There are certain spaces that are clearly Guy Turf. They are the zones designated for guy-only activity. For instance: the garage, the workshop, and the hardware store. Add the barbershop, the parts counter at an auto supply store, and for some unlucky guys, the uncomfortable chair outside a woman's dressing room in a department store. And for the really lucky guys, the inside of a mobile tool truck.

You just don't see women hanging out in these areas. That's because these are Guy Turf. Each is a special spot where a guy can celebrate being a guy. He doesn't have to dress up, be polite, or even shower. He can be himself.

When a guy is hanging out in Guy Turf, his testosterone levels increase (with the possible exception of the chair near the dressing room—guys tend to take naps there).

Guys hanging out in garages and workshops talk about tools and power. They like spending time there, picking up the fragrance of gasoline, sweat, and paint thinner—the ultimate macho cologne.

Tools have a special attraction to guys. I have seen guys who have pinup calendars of tools—not women, just tools. They grab fleeting moments in their garage just to fantasize about a new pneumatic drill. Their ultimate indulgence is a visit inside a mobile tool truck.

These are the customized trucks with chrome, custom paint jobs, and every tool imaginable (and some not), carefully arranged inside the air-conditioned and carpeted environment of the shiny truck. CAUTION: It is dangerous to enter such trucks with a credit card. In six minutes a guy can charge enough tools to pay for his three children's college educations at Stanford.

A guy can rule the roost if it's at the hardware store or barbershop; but if he's married, his turf does not extend to the bedroom. Why does a married guy's bedroom look like a girl's? I had expected our bedroom to be designed with input from me. Somehow I don't remember talking to Suzanne about the floral motif, the yellow and pale blue pastels. The color-coordinated bedspread, shams, throws, curtains, valance, towels, and nightstand doilies were not my choices. I didn't even know what a sham or valance was until I got married.

For all the macho posturing guys emit, we are sleeping in a room that looks like Barbie's.

What's a guy to do?

Unless you are Ken, learn to deal with it. We like to pretend that we are macho and in control; but in reality the bedroom is clearly women's turf. Now hand me that coaster. I don't want to get a ring on my doily.

THE MACHO GUY

In our culture, guys face a lot of pressure to be "macho." This is the traditional male image taken to extreme. It's masculinity on steroids. To be *macho* means:

1. Never let them see you cry.
2. Never let them see you fail. (Real men win.)
3. Prove your worth with achievement.
4. Don't depend on anyone but yourself.
5. Be aggressive. (Real men make it happen; wimps watch it happen.)

Sound familiar? It's so familiar it seems like truth. In reality, the macho image is a myth—something that is familiar but tainted with error. The pressure to display machismo is an urban myth. How much error needs to be in a myth to make it dangerous?

Just a little bit.

How much cyanide needs to be in your soda to make it dangerous?

Just a little bit.

If we are chasing after an urban myth that is tainted with false ideas, we are setting ourselves up to be deceived. The longer we chase the myth, the farther we will be from discovering true manhood. The popular culture's promotion of the macho man is an enemy to the identity God designed for guys. The Bible warns: "Don't copy the behavior and customs of this world, but let God transform you into a new person by changing the way you think. Then you will know what God wants you to do, and you will know how good and pleasing and perfect his will really is" (Romans 12:2 NLT).

A macho guy is chasing after our culture's false ideas of manhood. If he is able to attain them, he will have problems in relationships, because a macho guy, feeling strong and independent, thinks he doesn't need anyone.

Norm Wright calls the macho display "the great male cover-up," noting that

> [Machismo] is an extension of the hiding that began in the Garden when God came looking for Adam and Eve after they had disobeyed Him. This image that men foster and project is not only rooted somewhat in genetic male characteristics, but also largely developed by what is taught, portrayed, and reinforced in our society. We have developed unrealistic cultural role models in films, TV, sports and literature that capture the attention and adulation of men. . . .
> Men are taught by other men and society not to need anyone, to be independent. They are told not to appear weak. Men are taught that task attainment and completion are

more important than developing a relationship. And above all, don't ask for help.[1]

We face a dilemma. We know we shouldn't try to be the Marlboro Man, riding his horse alone, squinting into the sunset; but we don't like the other extreme either. Richard Simmons comes to mind. Now here's a guy who relates well to women, *but* . . . we really don't want to be like him. Did you ever notice? For a guy who spends all day working out, he still looks a little plump. Besides, I could never leave the house wearing those ridiculous shorts he wears.

Are those our only choices: Marlboro Man or Richard Simmons?

Rejecting the macho man ideal presents some problems. Besides being accused of being a Richard Simmons-wanna-be, you risk rejection and ridicule. Guys are afraid to lose status in the eyes of other guys.

They reason, *I will become a wimp. I will lose my masculinity.*

THE BALANCED CHRISTIAN GUY

There is an alternative. We don't have to hop on our horse and puff our way into the western sunset to be real men. We don't have to bounce around in nylon shorts, squeaking slogans to a room full of Lycra-attired women. The alternative is becoming the Balanced Christian Guy. "Christianity embodies all of the genuine male characteristics in a balanced and healthy way. Man becomes more masculine in Christ, not less."[2]

In fact, the guy who rejects the false macho persona becomes more of a real man. Masculinity is a natural and healthy reflection of God's design. The macho guy is presenting a distorted masculinity. His behaviors are an act to hide his weakness, uncertainty, and fear. Coming across as in control, aggressive, and capable are diversions to keep people from discovering his very real insecurities.

Being macho requires a guy to put on an act. In Christ, a guy discovers that he can be authentic. That's the plea of the apostle Paul: "Be honest in your estimate of yourselves, measuring your value by how much faith God has given you" (Romans 12:3 NLT).

We need to have an accurate picture of ourselves. Not too big, and not too little. The Balanced Christian Guy is tough but tender and totally honest. He's like the children who built a tree house. They decided to make it their club. A club must have rules, they agreed. They didn't want some kids getting too bossy while others got picked on. They decided to paint a sign and hang it inside their tree house:

> Nobody act big,
> nobody act little,
> everybody act medium.

This is Romans 12:3 in action. These kids wanted club members to be honest and balanced in their estimation of themselves. Good advice: "act medium."

TRAINING FOR BALANCE

Being a balanced guy won't come easily in our culture. We must counteract the pressure to be macho with biblical principles and ideals. It involves time, work, and change. In other words, "training."

Just like you work out and train your body to maintain physical balance; you need to train to balance your identity as a Christian guy.

It won't come naturally; it's more likely to come supernaturally. As Paul writes, we must seek, in Christ's power, to become godly: "Have nothing to do with godless myths . . . ; rather, train yourself to be godly. For physical training is of some value, but godliness has value for all things, holding promise for both the present life and the life to come" (1 Timothy 4:7–8).

God is committed to helping us develop balance in our lives. We don't have to do it all ourselves. That's the macho myth: If you want something done, do it yourself. For the Christian guy it's different: If you want something done, allow God to do it in you and through you.

See the difference? One depends on human strength and resources; the other depends on God's. That doesn't mean He doesn't use our skills; we just don't depend on them for results. In fact, sometimes God chooses to use our weaknesses instead of our strengths. Paul learned that he received power when he was weak and vulnerable. God told him, "My grace is sufficient for you, for my power is made perfect in weakness." As a result, Paul chose to "boast all the more gladly about my weaknesses, so that Christ's power may rest on me. That is why, for Christ's sake, I delight in weaknesses, in insults, in hardships, in persecutions, in difficulties. For when I am weak, then I am strong" (2 Corinthians 12:9–10).

This is the perfect Scripture passage for the recovering macho man. God's grace is sufficient for you. It's enough! You don't need to earn it or prove yourself. He is not impressed with your strengths. God doesn't need them. In fact, if they get in the way of what God wants to do, He may eliminate what you trust in. He is far more committed to developing your character than making you comfortable.

Join me in saying, "I am weak!"

Hey, come on; you didn't say it. Say it out loud, "I am weak!"

Did anyone look at you?

It felt good, didn't it? Refreshingly honest. No pretense.

Look at that verse again. "I will boast of my weaknesses." That is just the opposite of the macho approach. Macho guys hide their weaknesses. They pretend they don't have any flaws. In Christ, we can be liberated from the tyranny of pretending we are always strong. It's OK to be weak. Indeed, embrace your weaknesses—they are the backdrops that God will use to highlight His strengths.

TRAINING TAKES TIME

Training requires determination. Macho guys might be devoted to pumping iron at the gym. This has some benefit—"physical training is of some value"—but "godliness has value for all things" (1 Timothy 4:8). We need to be committed to training for godliness. The macho myth says, "Strong men have muscles." The truth, based on Scripture, says, "Strong men are godly."

Training for godliness requires time. We can't shortcut the process. Growth and maturity take time.

A student at a Christian college once asked the president of the college if he could take a shorter course than the one prescribed.

"Oh, yes," replied the president, "but then it depends on what you want to be. When God wants to make an oak, He takes a hundred years, but when He wants to make a squash, He takes six months."[3]

The apostle Paul was confident "that he who began a good work in you will carry it on to completion until the day of Christ Jesus" (Philippians 1:6). The apostle also declared that God will cause "all things to work together for good" (Romans 8:28 NASB). If you understand the growth process—if you know there will be barriers and are willing to learn the lessons from failure—you're more likely to learn how to turn the barriers into opportunities. In God's hands, that's exactly what barriers become. And that's exactly what the Evil One doesn't want you to know. Hang in there. Don't quit! [4]

A man confined to his bed with a serious illness one day observed on his windowsill a cocoon of a developing butterfly. As nature took its course, the butterfly began its struggle to emerge from the cocoon. The creature engaged in a long, hard battle. Hours went by, and the struggling insect seemed to make almost no progress. Finally the man decided to help. He took a pair of scissors and snipped the opening a little larger to help the butterfly. Then the butterfly crawled out, but all it ever did was crawl! The stress of the struggle was intended to push colorful, life-giving juices back into the wings, but the man cut this process short. Now the butterfly that was meant to fly was condemned to spend its brief life crawling in the dust.[5] Don't try to shortcut the natural process of growth.

DEVELOPING A BALANCE

We have discovered that the macho guy is suffering from a lack of balance. He is at one end of the spectrum. At the other end is the wimpy guy. We haven't talked much about him. I don't think we need to. We don't experience the cultural pressure to be wimpy: "Come on and let others trample over you. Don't stand up for what you believe in. Give in!" That's a message we never hear.

How do we develop balance? Balance is critical for many things we do in life. If we never balance our checkbooks, we can expect to have problems. Balance is essential for riding a bike, skiing, and even walking. Most of what we do in life requires balance.

To develop our balance in life, in an environment that changes almost constantly, we need to tap into the power available through God's Holy Spirit within us. As Paul explained: "For God did not give us a spirit of timidity, but a spirit of power, of love and of self-discipline" (2 Timothy 1:7).

To understand this resource, picture an old-fashioned teeter-totter. What happens if you are riding with a friend and he jumps off? Pain! And whether we are on the playground or in the boardroom, we need balance; without it, we suffer.

Got the teeter-totter in mind? On one end God has given us a spirit of *power;* on the other end is His *love* within us. In the middle is *self-discipline,* which is a fruit of the Holy Spirit (see Galatians 5:23). It looks something like this:

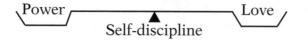

God has not given us a spirit of timidity (or fear). His Spirit equips us to take on life. God's Spirit prepares us; He balances us. There may be times when we need power. A situation that is challenging and overwhelms us will require God's power. A person who needs to be confronted will demand strength that we may not have in ourselves.

On the other end of the teeter-totter is love. Some relationships may require more love than we are prepared to give. There may be situations that demand our attention that we don't care about. This is when God's Spirit empowers us with love that is beyond normal human capacity.

We are fearful when we aren't prepared; but God's Spirit empowers us to take on life's situations, whether we need power or love. He also helps us to know which one we need and gives us the self-discipline to flow from one to another. In our quest to become balanced guys, we may need power to face something challenging, love to love someone who is unlovely, and self-discipline to know which to use. By God's Spirit we can "speak the truth in love." We don't have to be wimpy, and we don't have to be macho posers. We can be authentic. We can be balanced.

Guidelines for Real Guys

Principle 10: A real guy lets God's Spirit empower him with power and love. Through God's Spirit, he develops the self-discipline to balance power with love.

11

Climbing the Ladder

*V*isit the midway games at the county fair: You've just entered the hormone zone. Here squinty-eyed, sweaty guys in tank tops (with entirely too much back hair showing) are lined up, pitching baseballs at leaded milk bottles to win cheap stuffed animals. Dollars are continually pulled from their wallets, as the hardballs miss and smack the corrugated metal backboard.

The primal hunter-gatherer instinct kicks in and all sense of logic is lost. Another buck, another ball. *Must knock over bottle. Must win Elmo.*

As part of my psycho-sociological research for this book, I went to the county fair. With lab coat, clipboard, and laptop, I was equipped to do serious research. Not wanting to stick out, I wore casual shoes. I observed guys quickly spend over $50 on midway games in an attempt to win an obnoxiously huge stuffed animal.

This year, Elmo was the rage. I wondered where the extra copies of this purple, four-foot-tall, Sesame Street celebrity would be stored a week after the fair. It turns out that this fuzzy creature isn't what really motivates guys to ignore their girlfriend (who may be as gorgeous as a supermodel) to focus on smashing milk bottles.

According to experts, guys become obsessed with winning for two reasons: (1) ego and (2) brain chemistry.

EGO IN ACTION

Ego

We discussed a guy's competitive urge (called "the competitive reflex") in chapter 7. But some guys move beyond competition to sheer ego. They want to prove they are still athletes. They may be in horrible shape, but they still feel that they are "just a few pounds over their high school weight." Denial is dangerous. I watched more than one guy throw one too many and throw his arm out. Their minds might have said high school, but their bodies said forty-something.

A guy's ego can play games with his mind.

But what's this about brain chemistry? Our brains use chemicals to make things work. According to researchers, one of these neurotransmitters is called dopamine.

I think this is named after guys.

I can just hear the woman scientist who discovered this: "Oh look! A chemical that makes a guy do silly stuff. What should I call it? Hmmm . . .I know, I will name it after my husband, 'Dope of Mine.'"

Within years, it was shortened to "Dope o' mine."

Dopamine stimulates guys to be aggressive and hypercompetitive. They feel the rush and excitement. They must win at any cost. They must be successful with their quest. Even if it costs them $58 for a stuffed animal that is worth $12.

It reminds me of the rats we observed in college. Not the ones in the dorm, the ones in the laboratory. These persistent rodents would hit the pellet bar about fifty times just to get a food pellet.

Hit the bottle. Knock over the bottle. Get a prize. Win the adulation of the crowd.

"Wow! That guy in the Harley Davidson tank top just knocked down a milk bottle. He's quite an athlete! Look at that huge Barney he won!"

The pitcher's girlfriend kisses him. He hands her the purple dinosaur; she disappears behind it. He walks away from the venue feeling proud. *I have conquered. I am successful.*

THE QUEST FOR SUCCESS

Guys want to be successful, even if it is a meaningless endeavor like bagging a Barney. That raises another question about being a real guy: What is true success for a guy? Success isn't a destination we arrive at, as much as it is the direction we are journeying. It is found by following after God alone.

This contrasts with what we hear from our culture. We live in a culture obsessed with success that is measured by winning and doing. We have swallowed Vince Lombardi's slogan, "Winning isn't everything. It's the only thing." Guys are identified as winners or losers. There's a label we would hate to be stuck with. Nobody wants to be branded as a loser. Being called a "failure" is the ultimate stigma.

Real guys find real success by God's standards alone. As proof, consider the outcome of adopting the "winning is everything" philosophy. Guys obsessed with success become more vulnerable to the temptation to do whatever it takes to win: including deception, manipulation, cheating, and compromise.

What is success in God's eyes? Gary Oliver argues:

> From God's perspective, success isn't merely the absence of failure. He doesn't measure our value or worth in terms of our accomplishments. God measures our growth in terms of the development of Christlike qualities. He looks at success as a direction more than a destination. And He knows that an absolutely essential part of growing, maturing, and developing Christlike qualities involves stepping out in faith and risking failure.[1]

For the Christian guy, success is personal and spiritual growth. When we are growing to become more like Christ, we are successful. To comprehend God's definition of success requires a personal relationship with Him. The first step toward lasting success and significance is a vital, growing relationship with our Lord.

> "For I know the plans I have for you," declares the Lord, "plans to prosper you and not to harm you, plans to give you hope and a future. Then you will call upon me and come and pray to me, and I will listen to you. You will seek me and find me when you seek me with all your heart. I will be found by you." (Jeremiah 29:11–14)

When we know the Lord intimately, we come to know His custom plans for us. Plans with hope. Plans with a favorable future. As we grow closer to God, we discover what He wants to do in our lives and what He is up to in the world. It's always wise advice to find out what God is doing, and to join Him there.

CONNECTING WITH A HEAVENLY FATHER

When we seek God with all our heart, we will find Him. I think guys spend much of their lives in pursuit of connecting with their heavenly Father. They are desperately searching for affirmation and approval. When we face eternity, we all are eager to hear our Father in heaven say, "Well done, my good and faithful son. Welcome to heaven. I have been expecting you. Look what I have prepared for you."

Patrick Morley captures this kind affection in this letter from Father God to a man:

> You have wanted success. Success is elusive, isn't it? That's because you have been living by your own ideas. I do want you to be successful, but on My terms, not yours. You measure success in the quantity of your possessions and achievements. I measure success in the quality of your character and conduct. You are interested in the success of your goal. I am interested in the success of your soul. True success is to satisfy your calling, not your ambition. Live as a called man.

The biggest problem I see in your life is that you have spent your whole life looking for something worth living for. It would be better if you found something worth dying for. Give your life to that, and I will give you joy, no matter how hard the path becomes. What is the cause you would be willing to die for? Better still, who is the one you would be willing to die for? How, then, should you reorder your life?

I made you with dignity. I created you to be significant. I have put in you the spark of divinity. You are my crowning achievement. You are the full expression of My creative genius. You are my most excellent creation. I was at my very best when I created you.

Do you understand and believe what I have just said?[2]

Which are you more interested in? The success of your goal, or the success of your soul? As guys, we spend a lot of time and effort pursuing our goals. We receive applause for being "get-it-done" guys. But what about the growth of our souls?

Success is more than a completed checklist. It is more than efficiently accomplishing all of our tasks. Hit men can be very thorough and efficient, but that does not make them successful (at least not in God's terms).

When we are in a close relationship with God, He can even make our failures into opportunities for growth. In fact, we often learn life's deepest lessons through our failures. Maybe we are more teachable when we are down on our knees. "God uses many things to fuel the fire in the refining process of our lives, including our failures," notes Oliver. "Often it is through disappointment, discouragement and frustrations of failure that we learn to see through the eyes of the Spirit and develop the loving, patient and forgiving mind of Christ. God can use the light of failure to help us see beyond our flaws toward opportunities for growth."[3]

God is more committed to developing your character than your reputation. He is more interested in your refinement than your comfort. To make you more like His

Son will take some work. It will take some sculpting, chipping off some familiar, but unnecessary stony material.

PROFIT AND LOSS STATEMENT

God's definition of success is different than society's definition. His definition of profit is also different. Thus Paul found:

> Whatever was to my profit I now consider loss for the sake of Christ. What is more, I consider everything a loss compared to the surpassing greatness of knowing Christ Jesus my Lord, for whose sake I have lost all things. I consider them rubbish, that I may gain Christ and be found in him, not having a right-eousness of my own that comes from the law, but that which is through faith in Christ—the righteousness that comes from God and is by faith. I want to know Christ and the power of his resurrection and the fellowship of sharing in his suffer-ings, becoming like him in his death. (Philippians 3:7–10)

True success is knowing Christ and being vitally con-nected to Him. In Him we discover genuine profit—the kind that will last for eternity. In Him we become aware that what we used to consider treasure could now be considered rubbish.

True success isn't being perfect or keeping a set of rules; it's a relationship.

You can't earn this relationship. You can't win this re-lationship. You can't inherit this relationship.

You receive it as a gift.

That is what grace is all about. Grace is love in rela-tionship.

God wants to know you. He wants you to know Him.

What is success to you? A prestigious job with a huge salary? A new luxury car? A large house? A membership at the country club?

Paul would say, "I consider them rubbish, that I may gain Christ."

These things aren't wrong. (You can give me a new

Lexus!) They just aren't true indicators of a man's success. We don't need to have these things to be successful. We can be free from the tyranny of our culture that tells us we need stuff to be successful.

"I WILL CONSIDER MYSELF A SUCCESS WHEN . . ."

A friend of mine was on a flight to Tokyo. He was a successful designer for Mazda and going there on business. On the long flight, he jotted some personal goals. " I will consider myself a success," he wrote, "when I:

- am walking close with Christ everyday.
- am living out 'to live is Christ and to die is gain.'
- am building a strong and intimate marriage with my wife.
- am loving my kids with sacrificial love.
- am performing my job to the best of my abilities.
- am using all of my resources to point others to Christ."

A few weeks later, he was skiing and got caught in an avalanche. The snow buried him. He died, leaving behind a young wife and two children. At his memorial service, we reflected on his abbreviated life. Someone read his personal goals. We all agreed that even though our friend died way too soon, he had accomplished his goals for success.

THE PERSONALITY MYTH

Our society seems enchanted with externals. Popularity, possessions, status, and personality are the standards by which most people measure one another. Success becomes a function of marketing, image control, and perception. In our culture, success is external.

As a result, men have become bewitched by the externals. We focus on personality rather than character. Best-selling author Stephen Covey writes:

Shortly after World War II, the basic view of success shifted from the Character Ethic to what might be called the "Personality Ethic." Success became a function of personality, of public image, of attitudes and behaviors, skills and techniques that could lubricate the process of human interaction. This personality ethic essentially took two paths: one was human and public relations techniques, and the other was positive mental attitude.[4]

In our culture, guys are rewarded for personality more than character. In fact, in some cases, if you are a man of character you will be punished. Consider the "standard operating procedure" of some businesses, which bend the ethical line to maximize the profit margin. If you are an honest guy, you may find yourself in conflict with the corporate culture—and you may lose financially, socially, or vocationally.

Prior to World War II, Americans considered personal character a building block for success. Qualities such as honesty, integrity, humility, courage, loyalty, justice, patience, industry, simplicity, modesty, and the Golden Rule were the hallmarks of effective living.

But today's society shouts, "Image is everything!" The shift from the character ethic to the personality ethic has led us to become guys craving for image. Status, reputation, and position now determine worth. It's not who you are, but what you have.

The personality myth teaches that the goal is to be liked, so do what it takes to be liked. This obsession on externals forces us to focus on what we do rather than who we are. It makes us vulnerable to the opinion of others, and it often compels guys to strive to earn and achieve so they will have the goods that will proclaim their worth.

If our basis for self-worth is the personality ethic, we will be very insecure, because our security will be determined by the shifting opinion of others. The personality ethic is weak because it can't handle adversity. Adversity challenges its source of worth.[5]

The most tragic effect of the personality ethic is that it confuses the goals. The personality ethic says that the goal is to be liked. The character ethic says that the goal is to be like Christ. If a guy is operating on the personality ethic for self-worth, he may be tempted to do some things, which may be unethical or ineffective, but will net him popularity. If his goal is to be like Christ, he will desire to please God, even if it may not be the most popular option.

The character ethic realizes that God develops character in the lives of men who are open to the reforming power of His Holy Spirit. This relationship is critical for character development. In his classic, *My Utmost for His Highest*, Oswald Chambers reminds us of this truth.

> We must never allow anything to damage our relationship with God. But if something does damage it, we must take the time to make it right again. The important aspect of Christianity is *not the work we do, but the relationship we maintain* and the surrounding influence and qualities produced by that relationship. That is all God asks us to give our attention to, and it is the one thing that is continually under attack.[6] [emphasis added]

This is a pointed reminder for us workaholics: It's not the work we do, but the relationship we maintain. It's not wrong to work hard; just work hard at the right things. Work hard at your relationship with God. Work hard at your relationship with your wife. Work hard at your relationships with your children. Work hard at your relationships with the guys in your small group. And if you have any time or strength left over, go to work!

Of course I am overstating my point. But let's not forget *to keep the main thing the main thing*—and God is the main thing!

Relationships with those we love are a priority. I like that saying, "No guy at the end of his life says, 'I wished I would have spent more time at the office.'"

Which ethic drives you? The personality ethic or the character ethic? Consider the following chart to find out:

PERSONALITY VS. CHARACTER: TWO VIEWS OF SUCCESS

Personality Ethic	Character Ethic
Focus: What I do	Focus: Who I am
Depends on other's opinion	Not dependent on popular opinion
Driven for performance and perfection	Realizes that God gives character
Limited availability	Available to anyone
Quick to obtain	Slow process ofgrowth
Play the fool maintain questionable (even foolish) behavior to get attention	Not dependent on external success
Quick to lose	Persistent and permanent
God may take reputation away to build character	God will not take away character to build a reputation
Afraid of adversity	Survives adversity
Goal: to be liked (popularity)	Goal: to be like Christ (true success)

Source: Adapted from Tim Smith, *8 Habits of an Effective Youth Worker* (Colorado Springs: Chariot Victor, 1995), 58.

As this chart indicates, character counts. If we are basing our self-worth on the personality ethic, we will be insecure because our value is based on the opinions of others. If their opinions change we could be rejected. If our success is driven by the personality ethic, then our goal is to be liked. Popularity is the goal. Our ambition becomes to be liked.

In contrast, the character ethic is not dependent on public opinion. It realizes that God gives character to anyone; not simply the popular, successful or wealthy. It doesn't depend on external success, but is a process of growth over time. The goal isn't being liked, but being like Christ. A self-worth based on character withstands adversity and the fickle currents of our culture. A guy with character isn't concerned about pleasing everyone. His focus is on pleasing God.

Guidelines for Real Guys

Principle 11: A real guy believes that true success is discovering what God is doing and joining God there.

12

Do Brides Come with Scheduled Maintenance?

*A*dam was the first single guy. This may be obvious to you, but has it ever occurred to you that there was zero dating potential in the Garden of Eden? I mean the animals were interesting; Adam could talk to them (like Dr. Doolittle), but they weren't very good conversationalists. Of course, some dates aren't either; but that's not the point. Adam was lonely. Each of the animals had a partner, but he didn't. God caused him to fall into a deep sleep; and while he was sleeping, God took one of his ribs and made it into a woman.

As a result, even today, women accuse men of "being in a deep sleep," and men accuse women of "being a pain in the side." By the way, there is no record in Genesis of Adam ever waking up; so women may have a point here.

From the creation of man and woman we discover that guys are different from women. Guys are made from dust and women are made from bones. My next book will be entitled, *Men Are from Dust, Women Are from Bones*.

Do you know Adam's first words when he first saw Eve, in all her perfection?

"Wo! Man!"

She has been called woman ever since.

Now let's be serious about marriage and consider what went right in that marriage union of Adam and Eve—and what went wrong. First, Adam did one thing right: He made Eve his main focus. God had made the spouse the primary focus, with a guy leaving his parents to join in a new relationship with the woman he loves: "For this reason a man will leave his father and mother and be united to his wife, and they will become one flesh" (Genesis 2:24). And that's what Adam did.

Of course, as the first man, Adam did not have parents; as the first woman, neither did Eve. But Adam understood the point of God's creation of Eve: The two would become one in purpose and devote themselves first and foremost to each other. There is an important principle in Genesis 2:24: Before you can connect with your wife, you have to leave your parents. Your wife didn't marry your mom and dad; she married you! This verse teaches that the marriage relationship has priority over other family relationships. It's difficult for a man and wife to have intimacy ("one flesh") if one of them is still emotionally connected to his or her parents. This verse is not saying, "Destroy your relationship with your parents." It is saying that the marriage must come first.

God knew that it would be hard for some guys to leave home without Mom; but if they didn't, it would be trouble.

God has instituted marriage as a primary relationship. It deserves our top priority right after our relationship with God.

Adam devoted himself to Eve. Yet in the midst of their close relationship, each partner allowed another to interrupt their relationship. One individual surely got between Adam and Eve: the serpent.

The crafty serpent slithered his way in between the first man and first woman. His strategy was to cause division, create doubt, and entice with greed. By getting between Eve and Adam, he was able to cause division. By raising the question, "Did God really say?" he created doubt. And with the enticement of a tasty treat and new knowledge, the serpent tempted Eve to want more. His strategy worked. He was able to put distance between woman and man.

Ever since the Garden, sin has alienated woman from man. And this is what has gone wrong in marriage. There was—and is—a loss of trust. There was a loss of intimacy. As a result, there was shame: "They realized they were naked; so they sewed fig leaves together and made coverings for themselves" (Genesis 3:7).

Ever since the Garden, men and women have tried to cover things up from each other. Men pretend that they aren't emotional and women pretend that a man's lack of compassion doesn't bother them. Sin leads to a lot of pretending.

Of course, Adam did the usual guy thing: he blamed his wife.

Their disobedience brought consequences. Adam experienced hardship and pain in his labor, and Eve experienced hardship and pain in her labor.

GARDEN TALK

As you read Genesis, you capture some of the dialogue; but it is not entirely recorded for us. I offer the following as a possible rendering of what went on in paradise. After the Fall, man had much work, yet not without reason. God, who is love, showed grace even in giving work (though the pain of labor was a consequence of Adam's sin).

"Why did He have to invent work! I mean every day there are things to do. My work is piling up! God, I—"

"Yes?"

"Who's that?"

"It's me, Yahweh."

"I didn't know you were there."

"I'm always here."

"I didn't know you were listening."

"I'm always listening."

"So . . . what do you want?"

"You are the one who called."

"I did?"

"Yes, you called my name. You said 'God.'"

"Oh, I guess I did. Well, tell me, why did you invent work? Couldn't you have made lounging my calling?"

"I made you in My image. I worked creating this place. You can work too. Besides, it's good for you."

"I have a more natural bent toward *not* working now."

"I have noticed. Ever since you fell for the serpent's trick and ate of the fruit, you prefer lounging to working."

"I just don't have the same job satisfaction that I used to."

"That is the sin talking."

"And the woman *You* gave me, she is starting to look a little wrinkled."

"That is the sin settling."

"I just don't feel that close to her anymore."

"That is the sin rationalizing."

"Why do you keep saying *that?!*"

"Because it is true. I want you to understand the consequences of your disobedience."

"Hey, I was kicked out of the Garden; isn't that enough?"

"Your disobedience results in laziness, alienation, and a lack of concern."

"Are you talking about us? Me and You?"

"I am talking about our relationship and your relationship with your wife."

"Are you saying I am lazy, alienated, and cold about Eve?"

"Yes."

"Ouch."

The truth hurts, and God is truthful. Adam could have had the above conversation with God. And if Adam took advantage of asking God how he could improve his fractured relationship with God and Eve, the conversation might have proceeded like this:

"Well, what do I need to do to restore the relationship?"

"Realize that relationships take work. Your most important work is your relationship with Me and your wife."

"It is up to me? Why can't she do something to help?"

"Don't start blaming her again. You are quick to become defensive."

"I'm not defensive!" (Pause)

"OK," agreed Adam, "maybe a little. What should I do?"

"Take the initiative to care for her and show understanding. In other words, love her."

"How can I show Eve I love her?"

"Demonstrate understanding by listening to her. Not listening to offer advice or correct her, but to really understand her. Show her respect by accepting her feelings and valuing her opinion. Affirm her as much as possible. Reassure her that you enjoy her and enjoy time with her."

"So my solutions and suggestions aren't that helpful?"

"Remember, women want interactions, not solutions."

HER NEEDS

As we have emphasized earlier, men and women have different needs. With sin and selfishness interrupting our relationships, how can we men meet our wives' needs? When it comes to maintaining our cars, the car manufacturer offers schedules for maintenance. The automaker tell us exactly what to do to keep our cars safe and running well. Wouldn't it be great if God gave us scheduled maintenance for our wives?

He does. And His Word tells us her greatest need is

for unconditional, abundant love: "Husbands, love your wives, just as Christ loved the church and gave himself up for her" (Ephesians 5:25).

Christ loves continually (every day). Christ loves unconditionally. Christ loves with sensitivity. Christ loves sacrificially.

This is God's standard for loving our wives.

Marriage counselor Gary Chapman writes in his best-seller *The Five Love Languages:*

> We each come to marriage with a different personality and history. We bring emotional baggage into our marriage relationship. We come with different expectations, different ways of approaching things, and different opinions about what matters in life. In a healthy marriage, that variety of perspectives must be processed. We need not agree on everything, but we must find a way to handle our differences so that they do not become divisive. With empty love tanks, couples tend to argue and withdraw, and some may tend to be violent verbally or physically in their arguments. But when the love tank is full, we create a climate of friendliness, a climate that seeks to understand, that is willing to allow differences and to negotiate problems. I am convinced that no single area of marriage affects the rest of marriage as much as meeting the emotional need for love.[1]

Our hearts cry out to be loved by another. Women need love. And we men need love too.

That's OK. You can still be a guy and need love. Alienation and isolation are painful. God created us to relate to each other and be intimate with our wives. We have an intense internal desire to know and to be known. Marriage is God's design to meet our needs for intimacy and love.

But sin separates us. It separates us from God and each other. *Sin* is a biblical word for the mess we are in. Thankfully, Jesus came to earth to restore our relationship with God and other people. The cross is vertical and horizontal, reconciling us with our Father and our brothers and sisters.

Sin makes us look at life with blinders. Author and pastor Gary Kinnaman describes sin's destructive power and God's original purpose:

> Sin is endemic.
> Sin is the root of racism.
> Sin is the root of sexism.
> Sin is the reason why we all can't just get along because it's the perversion of relationship as God originally intended it in Genesis 1:27: "So God created man in his own image, in the image of God he created him; male and female he created them."
>
> This little poem-like statement is what Bible scholars call "Hebrew parallelism", which links the ideas of each of the parallel statements. Here in Genesis 1:27 it means that the image of God is both male and female. *Both!* In other words, it takes both man and woman—all of us together—to fully represent and experience God. It was never God's intent to create a cult of individuals—little dribbles of humanity, isolated in their private lives by private interests, divided by gender and racial hostilities. . . .
>
> Well, why can't we just get along?
>
> Well, we can't . . . without Jesus. When you are in the middle of a maddening puzzle of irreconcilable problems, your only option is to turn to Jesus: "For he himself is our peace, who has made the two one and has destroyed the barrier, the dividing wall of hostility . . . through the cross, by which he put to death their hostility" (Ephesians 2:14–16).
>
> Difference is divine, Godlike. It comes right from God. To value difference is to honor God. But because sin is endemic, we turn our differences into war zones.[2]

Marriage doesn't have to be war. It can actually be enjoyable! We can embrace our differences, with God's help. Then we will express our gratitude to God for His creativity.

MARRIAGE MYTHS

Some problems occur in marriage because we don't value or accept our differences. We pretend we aren't different, or we persistently pursue trying to change what is different in our spouse. As Kinnaman notes, "Difference is divine. . . . To value difference is to honor God." We have a creative God. He likes to make things different. Aren't you glad He didn't make all of us alike? How boring!

Sometimes our perception of marriage is tweaked by our biases. Some of us grew up believing myths. Those myths may be familiar, but they are false. At times they contain a kernel of truth, but they are largely lies. Destructive lies. Disappointing lies.

For instance, many men and women believe in the fairy-tale romance, which is supposed to end with, "And they lived happily ever after." That may work for fairy tales, but not for real life. But at some levels we believe it.

For the single man, a common myth is "If only I can meet the right woman, then I'll have a great marriage." Most of the myths about marriage begin with simple conditions: "If only . . . then." Here are several "if only" statements you may believe (and even utter on occasion).

"If only we could have a nice house, then . . ."
"If only we had kids, then . . ."
"If only my kids were . . ."
"If only we had more money . . ."
"If only my wife would . . ."
"If only I had a better job . . ."
"If only I got promoted . . ."
"If only I was retired . . ."
"If only I was healthy . . ."
"If only I wasn't married . . ."
"If only I was younger . . ."

Some people spend their life thinking about if-onlys. Those are unnecessary marriage myths. Drs. Les and Leslie Parrott in their helpful book, *Saving Your Marriage Before It Starts*, challenge us to face marriage myths with honesty. They identify four common myths:

1. We expect exactly the same things from marriage.
2. Everything good in our relationship will get better.
3. Everything bad in my life will eventually disappear.
4. My spouse will make me whole.[3]

These might seem familiar to you. You may have even quoted them to others, but they are dangerous myths. Your wife and you come from different families and life experiences; you are different genders. No wonder the two of you had vastly different expectations about marriage.

The good aspects of your relationship are not guaranteed to remain; they may fade with time. They might be replaced with annoying or harmful habits. Expecting what is good to get better is a misconception about marriage.

Similarly, expecting the bad to fade away with time is like hoping that the patch of dandelions in your yard will disappear if you just leave them alone for awhile. Things tend to wear down and get worse if they are left alone. Marriage is no different. It's a law of physics. The second law of thermodynamics states that energy tends to dissipate over time. Things go from order to disorder over time. This law of the universe applies to the energy and order of marriage. Over time, if left alone, a marriage relationship tends to deteriorate and lose momentum, energy, and order. If neglected, a marriage can die.

The final myth, "My spouse will make me whole," is also unrealistic. Expecting someone to bring healing, completeness, and meaning to your life sets you up for severe disappointment. Your spouse cannot make up for what is lacking in you.

I know some guys who reason, *My wife is the tender and caring partner. I'm the insensitive jerk. We complete each other.*

It doesn't work that way. If you are incomplete, you bring an incomplete person to the marriage. You can't expect your wife to make up for what is lacking in you. But you can do something about it. You can work on becoming more of a whole man. Even if your wife doesn't change, it will enhance your marriage, because you are bringing more wholeness to it.

FINDING TRUTH AND DIRECTION IN LIFE

We discover an escape from the myths in the enlightening pages of Scripture: "You will know the truth, and the truth will set you free," Jesus said (John 8:32). We discover wholeness in God's Word: "I have come that {you} may have life, and have it to the full" (John 10:10.) We discover direction in an intimate relationship with Jesus, who is "the way and the truth and the life" (John 14:6).

Truth. Life. Direction. Which do you need? Are you caught in some marriage myth trap?

What is the answer? To know the truth and to avoid the marriage and sexual myths of our culture, consider Gene Getz's advice in his classic best-seller, *The Measure of a Man:*

> We should fortify ourselves through regular study of the Word of God and prayer.
>
> Nothing dulls a desire for communication with God and the study of His Word so much as indiscriminate exposure to illegitimate sexual stimuli. And nothing is so effective in combating temptation and lust as an effective prayer life and Bible study program. Thus, the apostle Paul wrote, "Whatever is true, whatever is honorable, whatever is right, whatever is pure, whatever is lovely, whatever is of good repute, if there is any excellence and if anything worthy of praise, let your mind dwell on these things." (Philippians 4:8)[4]

Getz offers another antidote to marital and sexual myths: Be occupied.

> We must avoid unnecessary idleness.
> This was David's moral downfall! His temptation turned to lust and sin while he was busy doing nothing. When temptation is strong, idleness is pure folly. It has been the preliminary step to the downfall of many men, even spiritual leaders. [5]

How is your thought life? Is it pure? Do you peruse the Internet looking for pornographic pictures on certain web sites? What kind of magazines do you look at? Are you filling your mind with honorable images from videos? TV? Movies?

Is your mind programmed for excellence? Our minds require routine maintenance. It's like changing oil. Out with the bad, in with the new. Does your mind need an "oil change"?

HOW TO HAVE A CLASSIC MARRIAGE

For a growing marriage, we need to invest tender, loving care (TLC) in our wives. We need to "baby" them with sacrificial expressions of care—the same way we would "baby" a prized show car: polishing it, keeping it out of the elements, and fixing minuscule oil leaks. I can't imagine purchasing a beautiful car and leaving it out in the rain. It would be ridiculous to expect that the leak in the oil pan would fix itself.

Cars break down. Leather begins to crack. Internal combustion engines tend to leak. Expecting these things to not happen is senseless. Similarly, in marriage, communication breaks down, and relationships begin to crack. The internal stress builds over time.

Classic marriages, like classic cars, require our love and attention.

Our marriages require routine maintenance. We keep our cars running by changing the oil every 3,000 miles.

Are we as faithful to maintain the purity and care in our marriages?

Our wives need a fresh filling of honor on a regular basis. If our minds are focused on things worthy of praise, we will be able to honor our wives. For a classic marriage, we must practice routine maintenance, which means showing TLC to our wives.

Guidelines for Real Guys

Principle 12: A real guy understands that relationships require work. He chooses to work on his two most important relationships: with God and with his wife.

13

The Relaxed Father

*M*aking children is a lot more fun than raising them. Some men think their job is over once their wife becomes pregnant, but it's only beginning.

Let me ask you, "Why did you want a child?"

"Ah, well . . . ummh . . . because I wanted to have a son to play ball with."

"I wanted to have a daughter I could dress up in frilly dresses and have people notice how darling she is."

"I wanted to have a child to be a lasting replica of myself."

"Because my wife and I wanted a symbol of our love."

This last reason for having kids gets to me. Why do two reasonably alert, mature adults have to make another human to have a symbol of their love? It is like a project.

But kids are more than projects. They are people. I know this may come as a surprise to many of you dads: Your kid is a person.

Once we become fathers, we join the Dad's Club, a fraternity bound together with the mutual experience of bringing children into the world and having no clue what to do with them. Having a kid is different than a new power tool. The tool comes with instructions.

Bringing offspring into the world introduces men into a whole new world of expectations and responsibilities. We are expected to nurture our kids. This is new. For many guys, the last thing they nurtured was the sports car they had when they were single. Washing it

twice a week. Waxing it every weekend. Speaking loving-
ly to her as they caressed and polished the chrome. This
is nurture to many guys.

BONDING TO BABY

But what do you do with a cooing, oozing, live baby?
Suddenly, life isn't so simple. We are also expected to bond
with baby. For many males, this is confusing. When we
hear the word "bond" we think of the black, sticky stuff we
use to seal a head gasket. We don't like the idea of an adhe-
sive and our baby being used in the same sentence. But
now, dads are expected to bond with their baby.

As best-selling author and family counselor Mary
Pipher explained, while fathers in the 1950s weren't expected to hug their children, tell them they loved them,
or talk to them about personal matters, now men are expected to do all the things they did in the 1950s, plus be
emotionally involved. "Many fathers didn't learn how to
do this from their own fathers. Because they missed
their training, they feel lost."[1]

As a result, you may feel uptight. How can you become
the relaxed parent? By becoming prepared, of course. We
guys prepare by starting early in developing genuine relationships with our sons and daughters. (We'll discuss that
shortly.) We also prepare by realizing as guys that we can't
do it—nor need to do it—all by ourselves. Men can make
mistakes; fathers as men can make mistakes too.

Let's change our expectations and realize we don't
have to be perfect fathers. We can let others help us—our
wives, our friends, even a plumber.

THE FATHER FIX-IT FIGURE

For instance, fathers sometimes think they must be
the unerring Mr. Fix-it, taking care of every mechanical
problem. If you have great mechanical ability (are you
an electrician, plumber, or carpenter?), great. But if not,
don't sweat it.

Our culture is partly to blame. Society gives us—and our wives—great expectations about the male's mechanical abilities. We're to fix things around the house. We are supposed to pop out of the womb with a toolbox and a testosterone driven comprehension of mechanical engineering.

Women believe this, at least in my house.

"Honey, the sink has a leak. Can you fix it?" my wife sweetly asked.

"Of course, dear. I am a man. I have a tool belt."

It bugged me that she said, "Can you fix it?" She was challenging my maleness. She doubted my mechanical-testosterone capabilities. She was attempting to spread doubts about my inherent male-fix-it-ability. I decided to show her.

I crawled under the kitchen sink. My trained eye acutely assessed the problem: "A leaky sink" in laymen's terms. I also assessed that it was a sticky, dirty ant haven under the sink. We men are alert to these things. Sliding my way back out of the grimy cavern, I banged my trained eye on some metal gizmo. I tried not to yell; the kids were watching.

I carefully adjudicated the situation; it was time for a Trip To The Hardware Store. We men love it. It's male heaven. If we don't have a reason to visit the hardware store, we may be tempted to break something around the house so we can make our weekly pilgrimage.

For me, the hardware store is like a second home; they know me there. I walk in and I'm greeted.

"What'll it be today, Tim?" greets Sam.

"Leaking kitchen sink," I say proudly, as I saunter in. I say it loud enough so other flannel-wearing fathers can hear me. "Yup, got a leaker. Yeah, I'll knock this job out real quick, please the little woman, and get back to my real projects. Building a house, you know." I didn't bother to mention it was my daughter's dollhouse kit.

"So, what do you need to fix it?" asks Sam.

"Plumbing stuff."

"Stainless, copper, or plastic?"

Was I at the grocery store? Did he just ask, "paper or plastic?"

"Plastic." I hear myself say.

"Okay, the PVC plumbing is over here. What do you need? Elbow, flange, out-pipe, fittings?"

I froze. I didn't know a flange from a fitting. "It's leaking from that little bent thing on the bottom where it comes together with the other pipe."

"I know just what you need," interpreted Sam. "Here, try this. It's all in one kit. Everything you need is here. Just follow the directions carefully, Tim. They are on the back."

I don't like the way he said "carefully." What does he think I am?

"Oh, do you need some plumber's jelly?"

"Yeah, I think so. Sure." *What is plumber's jelly? Something to have on a plumber's peanut butter sandwich? Something to lubricate the pipe wrench? Maybe it's for the plumber's hands after they get bashed and smashed from working on the plastic thingamajig under the sink.*

"Don't want to run out of this stuff! Yeah, that plumber's jelly. What would I do without it?" I confidently jabber.

"Anything else?" asked Sam.

"No, that ought to do it."

Sam rang up the purchase. "See you soon, Tim."

I walked out of the hardware store sensing Sam's subtle sarcasm.

Back home, I soon descended under the sink and ripped out the old thingamajig pipe. By the time I got it out of the dank cavern and into the kitchen light, it had changed shapes. It now resembled a twisted and pummeled sea slug.

I had, once again, become a victim of Plumbing Magic. Plumbing Magic is common to all male homeowners. I'm not talking about the skill of adeptly repairing leaky sinks. I'm talking about how things change shapes and sizes. How the toilet water line metamorphoses from a 3/16 to a 5/16 on your way home from the hardware store. How the kit, no matter how complete it is, magically hides the right washer for the job.

I was no match for it. It was too strong to fight. Plumbing Magic is mysteriously strong, evasive, and a higher life-form.

I was devastated. I was no longer a man. I was a disappointment as a father-fix-it-figure. The part I had extricated from the hole didn't look anything like the part I had purchased. I had no clue what to do.

Women reading this might say, "Read the directions, you idiot!"

But I didn't hear you say this. I lunged into the kit with abandon. *I will make it fit. I am man—I will muscle it in!*

About three hours later, I announce to my family, "There we go, all done!"

Of course, no one was there. They got tired of the banging, crying, yelling, and wincing. They went to the mall.

It was the moment of truth. My maleness had been tested.

MALE PRIDE—AND THE FALL

Guys, when your maleness is tested, it's usually wise to back off. I know that this is difficult to do, but when we try to prove our maleness, when we try to prove our prowess, it usually gets us into trouble. Have you noticed the "only-I-can-do-it" mentality doesn't always lead to harmony in the home? It generally backfires because the focus is on us—what we think we can do in our own strength (real or imagined). When the focus is on ourselves, we are setting ourselves up. Pride comes before a fall.

We men hate to admit our needs. Yet that's who God

says we are—needy people who find peace in a God who sent His Son to meet our deepest needs.

For me, though, I was sure my maleness was in jeopardy, that I was about to be counted out by the referee. Just when I was about to throw in the plumbing towel, I heard the *Rocky* theme playing in my head. "Dah-dah-dah-dah-dah. Getting stronger . . ." I had met the challenge. I had taken on the altercation with the Plumbing Problem. Now, the verdict.

Nervously, I turned on the water in the kitchen sink. I was testing to see if it would leak. No, I was testing my male prowess. As a father-fix-it-figure, I was protecting my family from the wiles of leaking plumbing. Had I succeeded in maintaining the image of masculine mechanical superiority?

The "dah-dah-dah" from the *Rocky* theme song changed cadence. It began to sound more like "dop-dop-dop." To my horror and surprise, I discovered a leak. Not a small one. The thingamajig was leaking worse than before I started.

I glanced at my watch and decided on radical action: I reached for the phone. *If I'm quick,* I told myself, *the plumber can have this fixed before they return from the mall.*

Mind you, not once did I consider reading the directions on the back of the kit Sam sold me. After all, real men don't read directions. Real men don't ask for directions. Real men are adventurers. We would rather stay on the expedition (stay lost) then stop and ask for directions.

Stopping and asking directions is a challenge to our manhood. We feel we should innately know a map of the world. It's supposed to be built-in to our maleness.

Asking for help is admitting we don't know everything or can't do everything. It's an admission to our liabilities and limitations. It's a brush with reality. What happens if the word gets out that we are not capable at something? Like fixing the plumbing.

Within thirty minutes of arriving, the plumber had fixed the sink.

I was just cleaning up the mess when my wife returned from the mall. Wiping the grease from my hands, I proudly announced: "It's all fixed. It's as dry as the Mojave Desert. Doesn't leak a drop." I confidently packed up my toolbox. Hopefully, she'll never discover the plumber's receipt I hid under my pipe wrench in the bottom.

THE MECHANICAL FLU

By the way, the reason I'm mechanically challenged is because I missed one crucial day in high school due to the flu. Mr. Trevor Dale, my auto mechanics teacher, gave the *big* lecture. The *one* day I was home with the flu, Mr. Dale explained to the "lug nuts" in attendance crucial guy things:

- Turning to the right tightens things.
- Turning to the left loosens things.
- Water and electricity don't mix.
- Battery acid is not our friend.
- Don't clean the engine manifold with gasoline.
- Don't lick your finger and put it on the ignition coil.
- Stopping an automobile by slamming it into reverse is bad for the automatic transmission.
- Don't close the garage door and leave the engine running when you are installing new stereo speakers.

These are things I missed. I am functionally underempowered because of the flu. So don't expect me to be a mechanical genius. I suffer from chronic anxiety with my shame as a father-fix-it-figure.

RELAXING AS A FATHER

As fathers, we can relax; we don't have to do it all to impress our children or reassure our wives. Somewhere we picked up this idea that to be valuable we must be capable. To be capable we must know our way around—even in cities we have never been in before. I have news for you: That is unrealistic! It is OK to not know everything. You still have value.

The relaxed father will neither think nor act like he knows it all. In fact, such an attitude will interfere with one's fathering. Forget that approach, anyway. It won't work. Children have a way of showing us we don't know everything. The more we act like we do, the more determined they become to prove that we don't.

It can get embarrassing. Avoid turning red by being humble enough to admit you can learn from others. You can stop and ask for directions—directions for driving and for life. Besides, it provides a positive example for your kids.

Not too long ago we were on an expedition. In other words, we were lost. The whole family was in the car. They were watching—what will Dad do? I decided to give in. I pulled into the gas station and asked directions. Surprisingly, it wasn't too painful.

The smart father teaches and models that there is strength in true gentleness. That there is beauty in clear logic. That there is much thought in a beautiful masterpiece. This kind of balance will make you teachable. It will also make you approachable. An approachable dad is one who enjoys his relationships with his children. And that's how to relax and be yourself.

A REAL RELATIONSHIP WITH YOUR CHILDREN

Your children need to have a relationship with you. Your children need to connect with you. From you, your son will learn what it means to be a man. From you, your daughter will learn what to look for in a husband.

I know that word scares you: *relationship*. It may be what less-enlightened males refer to as a "woman's word." Conjuring up tea parties, tea cozies, tiny sandwiches, and silly, sentimental chat. Don't panic; we won't go that far!

One of the keys to all relationships is dialogue. We need time to talk *with* our kids, not simply *at* them. As we spend time listening, we will discover our children's interests. We can use this information to help build connections. It will take time. In fact, at times, it will seem like it is going slowly; but that's OK. Relationships with children grow organically; they can't be mixed in a test tube with some instant formula.

Children, like women, don't always need solutions. Sometimes they just need to connect, to know that we care. They will know that we care if we demonstrate awareness of their needs.

Weekly, ask yourself the question, "What does my child need?" His or her needs will change. Each child will need different responses from you at different times; try to stay current with your child's needs. We can serve our children by meeting some of their needs.

ENCOURAGE, COMFORT, AND URGE

The apostle Paul suggested some ways we men can influence our children in one of his letters to the Thessalonian church. There he compared his leadership to that of a father with his children: "For you know that we dealt with each of you as a father deals with his own children, encouraging, comforting and urging you to live lives worthy of God, who calls you into his kingdom and glory" (1 Thessalonians 2:11–12).

Notice the three different responses from the father: encouraging, comforting, and urging. *Encourage* means "to pour courage" into someone. It means to empower a person with boldness. At times, our kids need us to give them courage to take on a challenge.

Our children also need us to *comfort* them. This word means "to come alongside one who is hurting." It is a picture of a paramedic who rushes to attend to the wounded. As a loving father, there will be times your child needs your 911 response: not a lecture, but a loving touch.

The third response of a loving dad is the most direc-
tive. *Urging* has to do with motivation and direction. At
times, we may need to build a fire underneath our kids to
get them going. Urging is needed when our children have
forgotten to "live their lives worthy." If they are living for
themselves, and not considering others and God, then
we need to urge them to change. That is what discipline
is: creating stress in our kid's life in order to produce positive change.

A loving dad remembers that his kids aren't his alone.
They belong to God. A dad's job is to remind his kids that
they have a heavenly Father who calls them into "his
kingdom and glory." A loving dad urges his children to
keep God and His kingdom first in their lives.

When you think about it, it's amazing that God trusts
us with His kids. They are on loan to us. God is obviously
a God of grace if He lets men like us be fathers. So many
times we really don't know what we are doing. We make
it up as we go.

That is the tension, isn't it? Not knowing if we are
helping our kids or hindering them. But at least we have
a model of our heavenly Father, who encourages, com-
forts, and urges us.

Fathering can be perplexing. But you don't have to
stay lost. You can pull over and ask for directions. It's
OK; you are still a man. The relaxed father doesn't try to
parent alone. He knows when to get help. He knows
when to ask for directions. The relaxed father has more
energy because he doesn't have to spend most of it pretending he's perfect.

Guidelines for Real Guys

Principle 13: As a parent, a real guy meets the needs of his
children.

14

A Balanced Life

c - Balance

*T*he house was dark and silent as I pulled my dinner out of the microwave oven. I was starved. It was 10 P.M. and I was sitting down with my nuked potato. It had been a full day—speaking, counseling, leading meetings, and interacting. After fourteen hours of work, I was drained and irritable. I was glad that my wife had gone to bed—it probably saved an argument.

I munched on the steaming, cheesy potato and stared out the window. *I can't keep going at this pace,* I told myself. Somehow I knew my marriage and work and entire life were in for trouble.

As a father I was beginning to understand the need to model balance to my daughters and be available to them. I took a deeper look into my soul and wasn't pleased. Beneath the facade of church chat and holy hype was a heart that was cynical, aloof, and cold toward God. God was a stranger to me, although I referred to Him often. My kids seemed distant, though I professed that they were important to me. My relationship with my wife had become routine, necessary, and uninviting.

I knew I was in trouble. I had lost my balance.

Balance is vital for being a healthy guy. You and I need to know how to balance our work lives and our home lives, our professional lives and our personal lives.

For many sports, balance is crucial. I like to surf. To stay on the surfboard, you need balance. You can have a deep, savage tan and still not be a surfer. You may have an expensive surfboard and a wet suit and still not be a surfer. Without balance, you can't surf.

SURF DUDE

Like Sean, for instance. He looked the part of the surfing pro. He even spoke the lingo. And one day he offered to give me a ride to a local northern California beach.

"Dude, let's go early and grab some crankin' waves. We'll do dawn patrol and stop for some grindage on the way. Cool?"

"Uh, yeah," I responded slowly. I couldn't believe this guy. He looked like a clone of Jeff Spicolli—the surfer in *Fast Times at Ridgemont High*. He was an exact replica. Sun-bleached blond hair hanging in his eyes. Flamboyant Hawaiian shirt, totally unbuttoned. Baggy shorts and flaps. And the stereotypical, Hollywood lingo for a surfer.

"Awesome. I'll jam by about sixish."

"See ya." I watched him walk away with a cool-guy swagger.

Dawn came and found us loading up our boards on Sean's beat-up Toyota Corolla. Ancient surf racks had rusted to the gutters. A "Pray for Surf" bumper sticker accompanied a dozen others plastered to his car. A quarter inch of sand was on the floorboards. Seat covers from Mexico brought an international ambience to the interior.

"How 'bout some tunes?" Sean asked. Before I could respond, he popped in some surf music from the sixties. "This will get us stoked."

On our drive to Pleasure Point in Santa Cruz, Sean interrogated me. "How long have you been surfing?"

"Since I was fourteen."

"Where did you learn?"

"San Clemente. I grew up there."

"Cool. Ever surf Trestles?"

"Yeah, all the time. You?"

"Nah, not yet. But I am planning on going to Hawaii this winter. Wanna catch the big swells. I can't wait to surf Pipeline. I'm a goofy-foot. I saw photos of some dude surfin' a thirty-footer. I'm stoked just thinking about it. I gotta get me a gun—you know, the kind of board they use for the Pipe? I have a friend who knows a shaper . . ."

Sean rattled on about his surfing exploits. The longer he talked, the more intimidated I got. *This guy is going to be really hot, and I'll be choking. I am going to regret this. Why did I ever agree to go with this guy?*

We pulled up to Pleasure Point, and Sean switched off the ignition. He left the music on loud to help "get us stoked." Through the gray, morning fog I could see lines of waves rolling into the point. A swell had come during the night. Waves were breaking in perfect shape, six to eight feet.

Sean was staring. For the first time he was silent. All I heard was the crashing of the surf. It was a welcome change.

"Looks like we got a swell," I observed.

Nothing.

"Hey, Sean, let's go, it looks good."

"Yeah, sure . . . ahh. . .You gonna go right now or wait for the tide to come up?"

"I'm going now, before it gets too crowded." After all, we did get up at 5:30 A.M.

"I'll be there in a minute."

Normally, I wait for my friends and we paddle out together. But this guy wasn't my friend. I had just met him. I had been introduced through a mutual friend who said, "Tim, you should go surfing with Sean. He's really into it. He can take you tomorrow if you want."

Now Sean was fiddling with something in his car trunk as I stared at the inviting surf. I quickly pulled on my wet suit and waxed my board.

"I'll see you out there, Sean!" I yelled as I jogged over to the natural staircase carved into the cliff.

"OK. I'll be right out."

The smack of chilly water in my face awakened me like a Grande Latte at Starbucks. I speedily paddled out after a set, to get in position before the next set rolled in. The waves were overhead and crunching with thick lips into hollow tubes. *I don't want to get caught inside when a set comes.*

The aerobic exercise of paddling in cold water left me winded by the time I paddled outside. I was able to catch my breath just before the next set. I paddled into position, and took off on a steep, hollow right. It was a long and fun wave.

I paddled back out and noticed Sean. He was just entering the water. What had taken him so long?

He didn't time his entry. As soon as he got on his board to paddle out, a big wave smashed into him, washing him back into the rocks. He shook his head (like a cool surfer guy) and started again. The surf pummeled him. About ten minutes later he made it out to where I was. He was paddling like a wounded otter and out of breath.

"Got caught inside," he huffed.

"Yeah, I saw." *And this guy wants to go to Hawaii?*

"Dude, I think I need a longer board."

It sounded like he was making excuses, and he had not even taken a wave yet.

I noticed he wasn't sitting on his board, but lying on it. The water was cold, so it didn't make sense for him to be lying in it. He flopped around beside me, trying to catch four or five waves—missing each one.

I was having a great time—catching a long wave, carving turns, doing floaters, hanging five, and getting tubed. Then I'd paddle back out and get set for the next one.

Sean lay there looking like a piece of kelp. He drifted

back and forth, but never seemed to be in the right place at the right time.

He looks like a surfer. He sounds like a surfer. He even has sand in his car! What is missing?

I watched him between waves. He didn't know how to paddle his board. He didn't know how to sit on his board. In spite of all his jive, he didn't know how to balance himself.

Surfing is like life—you need balance to be successful.

Sean had no balance. He had the act down, but he was a poser. He couldn't surf because he didn't have balance.

Living life without balance is posing.

We pretend we have it together. We can do it all. Be successful at work, maintain relationships at home, stay in shape and volunteer at some worthy organization. But sooner or later, the different roles in our life become competitive.

How do we balance time between pressing work and family roles?

In my counseling, I often hear, "I can't keep up with the pace of covering all the bases. Things that are important to me aren't getting attention. The faster I hustle, the more out of balance I feel."

Do you ever feel that way?

Like Sean, in the pounding surf, you may need to learn one fundamental principle—balance!

SLOWING THE FRANTIC PACE

We acquire balance by starting slowly. Remember learning to ride a bike? My dad ran alongside me and steadied my bike by grabbing the seat. It gave me a sense of stability and security. We went slowly until I developed a sense of balance. Then I could ride faster and stay up without his support. At first, balance is slow to develop; but with time, balance can help you go faster.

But you have to start slow.

Pace and product are the cadence of the day. Our culture attaches value to busy people: "They must be important." Achievement is another source of affirmation in our culture. "Just Do It" is more than a slogan for shoes; it is a national creed. Consequently, we begin to believe we need to hurry up and do more.

We are conditioned to have everything instantly. We order our fast food from a speaker box and expect to have it prepared by the time we drive the thirty feet to the pick-up window. Automatic teller machines give us instant cash. Self-serve, pay-at-the-pump gas stations save us a minute from walking in to pay. Cable shopping networks offer us express delivery of products we urgently need (but didn't know about until we saw them on TV). We have a love affair with haste.

We don't seem to have the time to get balanced.

But this is nothing new. From the time man left the Garden of Eden, sin has refused to let us rest. Our frantic pace is a result of taking shortcuts in life. Sin is often masqueraded, but unmasked it's the urge *I want to have it all, now!* Our natural drives lead us to an overloaded life.

We need balance. It is a principle of life. When followed, we enjoy health, relationships, and effectiveness at work. To understand balance, consider its opposite—imbalance. An inner-ear infection can cause a lack of balance. A head injury can leave you in a fuzzy fog. An unbalanced checkbook can lead to bounced checks and service charges. An out-of-balance life is not comfortable.

SPINNING PLATES

The act probably first appeared in the circus, then in vaudeville. A guy spins plates on the tops of sticks—five, then ten, fifteen, even twenty plates. The guy dashes from plate to plate to keep them spinning, even as he adds another and another. Do you ever feel like you are spinning plates, trying to keep one from falling and breaking?

We have many roles to play: workers, volunteers, fathers, husbands, etc. Having different roles is not wrong. But how do you see your roles? In our western culture we tend to view our roles as separate compartments. Our work life may be completely separate from our home life. Our leisure time persona may be quite different from our church persona. Instead, they should be integrated, working together like plates spinning in unison.

However, we grew up that way—keeping things separated. We went to different classes to study different subjects. We never thought of integrating ninth grade science with eleventh grade history. We developed a way of thinking that was compartmentalized. As a result, we grew up with this "either/or" approach. Today we see our roles as completely separate from each other. We see our work separately from who we are at home.

COMPETE OR COOPERATE?

Compartmentalized thinking is stressful. By its very nature it is competitive. *Should I put time into that project at work or should I rest this weekend? Should I spend time with my children or with my spouse?* The either/or mentality is stressful because it forces us into a combative position. Choosing for means choosing against. It is a classic win/lose strategy.

If we take a deeper look, we discover that all of our roles are interrelated. They are integral parts that make up the whole. How we play with our kids is related to how we handle stress at work. Our values and priorities as individuals influence how we manage the financial decisions at work. A man is more than the sum of his parts.

In our western approach to roles, we think in terms of hats: "Now it is time to change my work hat to my play hat." Or, "On Sundays I put on my Christian hat; it is a different hat than my Saturday golf hat."

A more holistic approach is to view the person as integrated and interrelated. This is the way Scripture views presonhood. We have different parts of our being that are connected and influence each other. Balance is seen as a way of maintaining dynamic equilibrium.

This, by the way, is part of integrity—being the same through and through.

Notice that Paul didn't encourage the Christians at Thessalonica to get their act together at work or to volunteer more at the church. He talked about being blameless—from the inside out. "May God himself, the God of peace, sanctify you through and through. May your whole spirit, soul and body be kept blameless at the coming of our Lord Jesus Christ" (1 Thessalonians 5:23). A man of integrity is blameless. He is the same on the outside as he is on the inside. Cut him, and you will find the same substance at any level. Integrity means to be the same: It's quality and consistency all the way through.

A blameless man has permitted the God of peace to permeate his spirit. He has permitted God to break down any walls of defense or self-protection. He has invited God to reconcile his soul within itself and with his spirit. A man of peace is one who has experienced God's healing. His spirit, once incomplete, has been made whole. His loving heavenly Father has healed his soul, once wounded. His body, once driven by lust, now is regarded as holy and sanctified as a temple.

The Holy Spirit seeks to be at work in each of us, impacting every area of our life. He seeks to have every area influence every other area as an interrelated whole. This leads to maturity and balance. This is cooperation instead of competition.

When we have this synergy, it creates energy in our lives. We are no longer in competition with ourselves. Instead of win/lose, we are working with a win/win.

We can then look forward to hearing Jesus say, "Well

done, my good, faithful, and balanced servant. Enter into eternity with me."

I have found this perspective to be liberating. For years I was caught up in the win/lose competitive paradigm. "This is work; this isn't. This is ministry; this isn't." Then I discovered that this wasn't the way Jesus operated. To Him, everything was related. He didn't get trapped by the either/or mentality of the day. Several times the either/or guys tried to trap Him with a technicality and Jesus sailed through by adopting a both/and paradigm.

One of my favorites is when Jesus healed the crippled woman on the Sabbath (Luke 13:10–17). The self-righteous either/or guys complained, "You are not supposed to heal on the Sabbath. That is our rule!"

Jesus answered, "You hypocrites! Each of you unties your donkey to lead him to water on the Sabbath. Why not untie this woman from being crippled for eighteen years and set her free on the Sabbath?"

The either/or guys were humiliated. But the both/and people were delighted with all the wonderful things Jesus was doing.

SEEING THE BIG PICTURE

Either/or guys get hung up on the picky details. Both/and guys maintain a big picture, because it is shaped by eternity.

I had been an either/or guy. But I am learning to be a both/and guy. It is liberating! I had spent weeks writing my personal mission statement. I had agonized over the words. I needed something that would sum up my mission in life. Finally, I came up with something I felt comfortable with. "My mission is to lead a life of integrity and faith that will influence individuals and families to build their lives on God's timeless principles."

As I considered my PMS (see, guys can have PMS!) I thought, *What can I do to integrate this into every area of my life?* I prayed, "God, help me to integrate my personal mission statement into every area of my life—spirit, soul, and body. Make it the hub that influences everything."

COACHING AND THE BIG PICTURE

That week I was asked to coach my daughter's track team. It would mean practices daily and all day Saturday for months. My first inclination was to say no. But then I remembered my personal mission statement. I want to influence people toward God's timeless principles.

My old either/or attitude resurrected, and I heard myself enter into a debate: *This isn't part of your ministry. You are too busy. You are important. You will miss out on speaking opportunities. You will have to postpone writing projects.*

Fortunately, I also heard my new both/and paradigm respond: *You are a leader of youth. You can impact these kids and their families. It is an extension of what you do in ministry. See it as part of who you are, not something that you do. Besides, the most important child you may impact is your own daughter.*

I was hooked. I volunteered to coach the team. My new, holistic approach really helped. Daily, I had to leave an hour early from work, but I considered it an extension of who I was. I managed to get my work done because I was working in concert with myself. I was working effectively, choosing to do the right things.

Coaching now had become part of the big picture, as part of my personal mission is to help parents. As a coach of a youth track club, I met dozens of parents. It became a natural outlet for me to build relationships with them. I invited many of them to parenting seminars I was hosting at the church. Five of them came. They really appreciated the support and information. "I have never seen anything like this. Your church is so practical and helpful. Can I come to church?" asked one of the moms.

"Sure. Come this Sunday. I'll meet you and sit with you."

"Uh . . . Excuse me," one of the track dads cut in. "I think my wife and I would like to come too. Is that OK?"

"We'd love to have you." I was thrilled. This was exactly what was supposed to happen. As salt and light in the world, we are to season people toward the gospel and point them to the Light. It was working.

Hey, maybe those hours coaching track will have an impact.

At church that weekend our pastor presented the gospel clearly and asked for people to respond. Four parents (from the seminar) and two of their kids made first-time decisions for Christ. It's not always that way, of course, but we men can always honor our personal mission statement and leave the results up to God.

After the church service, I was talking to a mother and her daughter who had accepted Christ.

"I never would have come to church, but you coached my daughter and I saw something in you I liked. Then you invited me to the parenting seminar. I really needed help, so I came. Today, I found out that what I liked in you was Jesus. And so did my daughter. Thanks, Tim." She hugged me with tears streaming down her cheeks.

"Thanks, Coach," added her daughter with a tear-stained smile, giving me a bear hug.

Through this experience, I discovered that our natural roles grow out of our personal mission. I wanted to live out my mission and pass on a legacy through all that I do—even coaching track and field.

I also realized that each role is a stewardship. We are stewards of all that God gives us—time, talent, and treasure. We are accountable to Him for how we invest what He has given us. It isn't simply ours to squander, enjoy, and spend on ourselves. Moving from an attitude of ownership to one of stewardship is critical for a man seeking balance.

A balanced man is accountable for the impact of his life. He chooses to leave a legacy for those who follow. In the great relay of life, we don't have to hand off the baton of abuse, emotional neglect, debt, spiritual anemia, or an addiction to acquisition. We can pass on a legacy of health and balance, of dynamic equilibrium. We can create synergy among the roles of our lives, because we see them as callings from God. He then empowers us to live out our call—with passion and with balance.

Guidelines for Real Guys

Principle 14: A real guy is blameless because he has developed a sense of balance.

15
Me? A Spiritual Leader?!

I used to be a youth pastor, but the junior high lock-ins did me in. In youth ministry you hope that you will be a spiritual leader. You hope that you will make an impact. One day, I had the opportunity to find out. One of my former students talked with me on his break from medical school:

"Matt, it's good to see you. How is school?"

"Great. I am learning a lot."

"I'm glad to hear that. I knew you would do well."

"Thanks. Yeah, I am, and you had something to do with that."

"I did?" I responded with curiosity.

"Yeah, it was your youth ministry that left its mark on me."

I was flattered, and I wondered what had helped him. Was it my inspirational teaching? My innovative programming? The adventurous retreats? Or my life-shaping leadership skills?

"It did?" I replied. "What was it that influenced you, Matt?"

"I don't remember one lesson. Sorry."

Six years in my ministry and he can't remember one lesson?

"Not one?" I asked.

"Nah, but I do remember you teaching me to windsurf."

"Me too. That was fun."

"What really impacted me was your desire to have fun."

"You're kidding!"

"No, really. You weren't uptight like other pastors and spiritual leaders I knew. You seemed so normal. I wanted to spend time with you. I wanted to be like you. . . .You even trusted me with your sailboard! That made me feel you had confidence in me. That is what I remember."

I was feeling ambivalent. On one hand, I was glad that I had left some kind of positive impression on Matt. The Lord knows I had spent enough time with the guy. But the things I had thought would have left an imprint didn't. All of the interesting lessons, all of the counseling sessions, all of the trips and meetings didn't do what I assumed they would do.

Did Matt actually benefit the most from our *fun together?* I would have never guessed that teaching a teen to sailboard would be a positive mentoring strategy.

The words resonated in my mind hours after I said good-bye to Matt: "You seemed so normal. I wanted to spend time with you. I wanted to be like you."

Wow!

Whether it's toward our children, wives, coworkers, or just good friends, we can become spiritual leaders, influencing those we know and love toward godly action.

We want to be influencers. We want to make an impact. Guys, we can choose how we will influence. Will we be shapers toward the Spirit or toward the flesh?

THE EXAMPLE OF CHRIST

I tried to figure how I had become a model for Matt.

Maybe I was kind of an example of Christ to Matt. It's a good thing he didn't see me twenty-four hours a day! Imagine, me—an example? OK, maybe I could be, in some limited way. Obviously, it wasn't in my teaching! But perhaps it was in the fun. I am thinking here of the times Christ showed *His* sense of fun. Consider:

- He helped to celebrate a friend's wedding by changing water into wine.
- He threw a picnic for five thousand potential "clients" after an important message.
- He walked on water.
- He had social times with people of questionable reputation.
- He created instant breakfast on the beach (see John 21:3–12).
- He laughed at death as He left behind an empty tomb.

Just when the legalistic religious community thought they had gotten rid of the young, controversial prophet, He defeated death and showed up to prove His point!

As the angel declared in triumph, "He is not here! He is risen!"

He truly is the Son of God.

I think that is fun. Victory is fun. Beating Satan at death is just a hoot! Defeating sin and death is something to celebrate.

As Jesus declared to all who would listen, "The truth will set you free" (John 8:32). Now that's fun! As believers, we have both: truth and freedom. We have much to be grateful for. Just make sure that you give your face notice that your heart is glad.

SPIRITUAL LEADERSHIP

Don't wince. I know that the topic of spiritual leadership can produce nervous tics with guys: quivering heads, blinking eyes, instant tension headaches, and a sudden urge to go to the men's room. If you have been around the church for a while, and you are married, you will have heard: "The husband is to be the spiritual leader of the home."

What do they mean by this?

You say, "That's why I bought the book. You, the author, are supposed to have the answers."

Well, first a disclaimer: I do not totally understand what the phrase *spiritual leadership* means. In fact, the phrase is not in the Bible; but the Bible does offer some guidelines on how to be a leader by being spiritual.

I'll get to those guidelines soon, but let's first consider some myths about spiritual leadership:

1. Spiritual leadership is being perfect.
2. Spiritual leadership is exercising your spiritual gifts.
3. Spiritual leadership is quoting Scripture.
4. Spiritual leadership is going to my men's group and men's events.
5. Spiritual leadership is being successful at work.
6. Spiritual leadership is having an admirable reputation at church.
7. Spiritual leadership is dressing and acting conservatively.
8. Spiritual leadership is having your wife and kids under control.
9. Spiritual leadership is being very active at church.
10. Spiritual leadership is having no problems.

These are cultural fabrications of what it means to be truly spiritual and an authentic godly leader. What do these myths have in common? They focus on the externals. They are more concerned with reputation, behavior, and image than character, heart, and intimacy with God.

Read the list again. Do they sound familiar? Has anyone given you advice using one or more of these? I think I have had some of these myths get to me.

The Scriptures, however, make one thing clear: if you want to be a spiritual leader, be like Christ. Paul described the spiritual man (and woman) as having the mind and attitude that Jesus had:

If you have any encouragement from being united with Christ, if any comfort from his love, if any fellowship with the Spirit, if any tenderness and compassion, then make my joy complete by being like-minded, having the same love, being one in spirit and purpose. Do nothing out of selfish ambition or vain conceit, but in humility consider others better than yourselves. Each of you should look not only to your own interests, but also to the interests of others. Your attitude should be the same as that of Christ Jesus: Who, being in very nature God, did not consider equality with God something to be grasped, but made himself nothing, taking the very nature of a servant, being made in human likeness. And being found in appearance as a man, he humbled himself and became obedient to death—even death on a cross! (Philippians 2:1–8)

IT TAKES TIME (A PROCESS)

Christ's actions contrast sharply with the list of ten myths about spiritual leadership. God's way to spiritual leadership is through humility, sacrifice, and esteeming others. God's way is a process. It takes time to mature spiritual leadership; you can't manufacture it overnight. There isn't a formula for spiritual leadership.

"As I reflect on my own life as a Christian, I can remember trying most of these formulas (myths), but usually with a certain degree of disappointment in the results," wrote Pastor Gene Getz in *The Measure of a Man*. "I have come to realize there is no quick shortcut to 'becoming a man of God'. . . All of us, of course, embark on our Christian journey with a variety of backgrounds and experiences—which affect the progress we make in our Christian life. But one thing is sure, no matter what our spiritual and psychological heritage, it takes time and effort to become a man of God.[1]

Would you recognize a spiritual leader if you saw one? He may not look like you would expect. A man of God, or, for this book, a guy of God reflects Jesus Christ in his total lifestyle. He demonstrates spiritual growth and development over a period of time. It is a process. Remember: process, not perfection.

IT TAKES SCRIPTURE (REFLECTION)

How can a guy develop these qualities? Let me tell you what has worked for me and dozens of men I know: the Bible.

Yup, that's what you need—a Bible. Get together with a small group of guys to work through the qualities of spiritual leaders listed in First and Second Timothy and Titus. Read a verse and discuss your definitions for the quality of spiritual leadership, and how to live it out in your lives.

For instance, in 1 Timothy 3, the first quality listed is "above reproach." What does that mean? What does a guy look like who is "above reproach"? *Reproach* is not a word that we use now. To be "above reproach" means to have a good reputation. A guy with a good reputation is living in harmony with biblical principles. He receives favorable feedback from godly friends. His circle of friends expands as they hear about his sterling character. Many come to confide in him. He is asked to take on challenging roles and tasks. You can have confidence in a guy with a good reputation.

IT TAKES ACCOUNTABILITY
(A GROUP OF MEN)

I began meeting with guys in small groups in 1977 with the purpose of our spiritual growth. We learned to ask the hard questions. We earned the right to. Some of those guys were young men then. I have lost count, but at least thirty of the guys I have met with over the years are now in some form of full-time Christian service. I am proud to pass on the torch. It makes me feel that I have had some significance. I want to make a difference. How about you?

A group can help you and other men to heed Paul's advice to Timothy : "And the things you have heard me say in the presence of many witnesses entrust to reliable men who will also be qualified to teach others" (2 Timothy 2:2).

IT TAKES DIALOGUE WITH GOD (PRAYER)

Meeting with a small group of guys for accountability and study of God's Word will help you become mature in your faith. But you need a daily dialogue with God to change your life.

If you were to receive a call from the world's richest person, would you take the call? Of course you would. If he asked you out to dinner at an exclusive restaurant, would you go? Of course you would. If he asked you to visit his luxurious yacht, would you go? Of course you would. Now here's the point: Would you be different after you experienced this splendid day? Would you tell others about what happened?

Of course you would.

God, the richest, wisest, kindest Being is calling. Do you take the call?

He is asking you to enjoy a lifetime of dining at a bountiful spiritual banquet. Do you go?

He has invited you to "re-create" with Him—to enjoy the lavish luxury of His grace, just for fun! Do you accept?

To enjoy God's benefits and to know Him intimately, we must talk with Him. An intimate, authentic dialogue with God will influence us to godliness.

Kent Hughes describes how a dialogue with God—through prayer—can impact a guy's character:

Prayer is like a time exposure to God. Our souls function like photographic plates, and Christ's shining image is the light. The more we expose our lives to the white-hot sun of His righteous life . . . , the more His image will be burned into our character—His love, His compassion, His truth, His integrity, His humility.[2]

When we dialogue with God, we gain confidence in Him. We learn that we really can trust Him. We learn to relax in Him. The concerns that used to bring us anxiety have been replaced. We have new concerns, but without the anxiety. We develop His perspective.

Connecting with God through prayer changes us. It changes our priorities. It changes our focus.

This could be why some guys don't like to pray. They don't want to be changed. They don't want to be vulnerable. They don't want to lose control.

> Perhaps some men have difficulty with prayer because they are take-charge, type A, aggressively masculine personalities. In contrast, prayer requires that we let God take charge. Prayer is not a time when we dictate to God. It is a time when we allow ourselves to be changed into what He wants us to be. Prayer is fellowship with God. We don't pray to change God's mind; we pray to understand what His mind and will are for us.[3]

IT TAKES HUMILITY (BEING SERVANTS)

Someone once told me, "We don't pray to change God's will. We pray for Him to change our will." Here again, we are to be humble servants (Philippians 2:1–8). A willingness for God to change our will indicates genuine humility.

Humility is probably the vital first step for a man to become more godly. A man cannot come to God proud and full of himself. He needs to come broken, honest, and humble. He needs to come with the same spirit Christ demonstrated as he sweat drops of blood in Gethsemane, "Father, not My will but Yours be done."

Like Jesus in Gethsemane, we need to be:

- Intimate
- Vulnerable
- Desperately real

Jerry Bridges writes about humility in his book *The Practice of Godliness:*

> Humility opens the way to all other godly character traits. It is the soil in which the other traits of the fruit of the Spirit grow. Humility manifests itself in our relationships—to God, to ourselves, to others. We are to be humble toward God and His Word, humble in regard to trials and blessings that come our way or abilities and achievements with which we are blessed, and humble toward other people. Humility is the proper attitude with which to approach all these relationships and circumstances. [4]

THE PRACTICE OF HUMILITY

Humility is difficult for us guys. We do pride so naturally; it comes with the territory. Arrogance is applauded by our culture. Humility is often viewed as a sign of weakness. Yet humility is our first step toward spiritual leadership.

As Bridges noted, humility before God will affect all of our relationships. When we are aware of our sinful and puny selves before a holy and almighty God, we will not self-righteously compare ourselves to others. We will not get caught up in petty issues. We can be humble in our relationships with other people because we have humbled ourselves before our heavenly Father. This is critical: We cannot experience humility in any other relationship until we experience a sobering and penetrating humility before God.

How do we develop humility? Practice.

As anything valuable in life, it will take some learning, some effort, and some trial and error. Let me suggest three qualities to practice to develop humility in your life:

1. *Teachable.* A humble guy is teachable. He is humble enough to admit that he doesn't know it all. He desires to be a lifelong learner. A humble guy can submit to instruction, correction, and rebuke, because he needs it. He is more concerned about maturing than being right.

The apostle Peter wrote, "Young men, in the same way be submissive to those who are older. All of you, clothe yourselves with humility toward one another, because, 'God opposes the proud, but gives grace to the humble'" (1 Peter 5:5).

2. *Honoring others.* A humble guy honors others. He places them above his own concerns, needs, or position. He has his ambition in check. He doesn't need to work people to get what he wants. He demonstrates honor by not manipulating people. The Bible says to "honor one another above yourselves" (Romans 12:10) and to "consider others better than yourselves" (Philippians 2:3).

Jesus told a story about a man who went to a banquet and grabbed a seat at the head table, only to be asked to move to a less honorable spot (see Luke 14:7–11). He warned us not to honor ourselves—it tends to catch up with us. A humble man will honor others before himself. He won't be concerned with being first in line at the market or first in line in the fast lane on the freeway. He doesn't have to assert himself at the expense of others. A humble man demonstrates honor to others by considering their interests above his own.

3. *Serving others.* A humble guy serves others. It's like the song says, "If you want to be great in God's kingdom," you gotta be a servant of all. That's based on Jesus' words in Mark 9:35. Jesus set the pace with service.

On the night of His betrayal, when He understandably might be preoccupied with His own fears about His impending death; Jesus focused on His disciples. He didn't focus on their dinner, their jobs, or their heads. He focused on their feet!

He washed their dirty, sun-cracked, and callous feet. This is the intersection of Christ's theology with His biography. He said he did not come to be served but to serve (see Matthew 20:28). After washing His followers' feet, Jesus explained, "I have set you an example that you should do as I have done for you. I tell you the truth, no servant is greater than his master, nor is a messenger greater than the one who sent him. Now that you know these things, you will be blessed if you do them" (John 13:15–17).

With this one act of service, he summed up a lifetime of sermons. True greatness in God's kingdom does not depend on possession, position, or popularity. True greatness in God's kingdom is in serving one another.

WAYS TO PRACTICE HUMILITY

C. Humility

God's blessing isn't in the knowing; it's in the doing. Here are some suggestions to help you do something to practice humility on your quest for spiritual leadership. Do these, and you will become a learner, a servant, and one who honors others. And you will be practicing principles for spiritual leadership. We begin with ten *suggestions for becoming teachable.*

1. Let someone else have the choice for the next movie, video, or restaurant.
2. Instead of doing what you would like to do for the weekend, submit your desires to your wife's.
3. Ask someone close to pray with you for God to show what He wants to teach you.
4. Tell someone thanks for correcting you.
5. When you encounter someone who thinks differently than you, don't judge him or her. Instead, try to understand his or her point of view.
6. Tour a museum or try a new hobby.
7. Take a class in adult education at the church or the community center.
8. Keep a journal. Review it monthly to see what learning God has brought to your life.
9. Develop a relationship with a guy who is from another ethnic, racial, or denominational background.
10. Spend ten minutes individually with each person in your family—listening!

Here are ten *ways to practice honoring others:*

1. Keep a list of your wife's and children's birthdates and gift ideas.
2. Discover the family's favorite ice cream and surprise the family with it.
3. Keep a prayer list for your family and friends. Keep it current. Let them know you are praying. Ask for updates.
4. Show interest in the hobbies and pastimes of others. Make a point to ask them about them.
5. At least once a year, write a note of appreciation to those who have contributed to your spiritual development.
6. Write a letter of appreciation and honor to your parent(s).
7. Develop a rite of passage for each child at key monuments in their lives. Give them a gift that symbolizes your honor and love for them, such as jewelry when they get baptized. (For more ideas, see *The Heritage,* by Otis Ledbetter and Kurt Bruner and *Family Traditions,* by Ledbetter and Tim Smith.)
8. Pass on a spiritual heritage to your child in the form of a blessing. (See *The Blessing,* by Gary Smalley and John Trent, for ideas.)
9. Express appreciation to your wife by celebrating your anniversary with a creative date or a weekend away. Time alone to focus on her honors her.
10. Honor the guys in your small group by coming regularly, keeping confidences, and diligently praying for them.

Here are ten *ways you can serve* your family and others:

1. Quietly, without anyone knowing, complete the most disgusting chore at your house.

2. Volunteer to clean up, paint, or do yard work at your church.
3. Commit to discovering your spiritual gift. Start by studying Romans 12, 1 Corinthians 12–14, and Ephesians 4.
4. Find a place to serve by using your spiritual gift. You may find yourself doing home repairs for single moms, working with children at your church, showing compassion for those in the hospital, or serving someplace else.
5. As a family, adopt a needy child from a foreign country. (Compassion International and World Vision are excellent ministries.)
6. As part of a small group, volunteer to serve at your local rescue mission.
7. Ask one of your wife's friends to invite her to brunch. While the two women are gone, clean the house.
8. Consider a family service project. (Habitat for Humanity is a reputable house-building ministry.)
9. Choose elderly people and make them baskets for their birthdays and holidays.
10. Volunteer at your child's school. Kids need role models of men serving.

True greatness in God's kingdom comes by serving others. Don't just be a guy, *be a great guy!* Get out there and serve. It's part of the stuff that makes you and me real guys.

Guidelines for Real Guys

Principle 15: A real guy will submit humbly to God's process of growing through serving.

Notes

Chapter 1: "You Are What You Do"

1. H. Norman Wright, *What Men Want* (Ventura, Calif.: Regal, 1996), 42–43.
2. Patrick M. Morley, *The Man in the Mirror* (Brentwood, Tenn.: Wolgemuth & Hyatt, 1989), 9.
3. Ibid., 25.

Chapter 2: A Real Man

1. Patrick M. Morley, *The Man in the Mirror* (Brentwood, Tenn.: Wolgemuth & Hyatt, 1989), 116–17.
2. Ibid., 274.

Chapter 3: Is *Integrity* a Car?

1. Laurie Beth Jones, *Jesus CEO: Using Ancient Wisdom for Visionary Leadership* (New York: Hyperion, 1995), 19.
2. Lawrence O. Richards, *Expository Dictionary of Bible Words* (Grand Rapids: Zondervan, 1985), 128–29.
3. Stephen R. Covey, A. Roger Merrill, and Rebecca R. Merrill, *First Things First* (New York: Fireside/Simon & Schuster, 1995), 185.
4. Charles W. Colson, "A Man and His Integrity," in *Go the Distance*, John Trent, gen. ed. (Colorado Springs: Focus on the Family, 1996), 100.

Chapter 4: Wimp or Warrior?

1. Gordon Dalbey, *Healing the Masculine Soul* (Dallas: Word, 1988), 180.
2. Ibid.

3. Joseph M. Stowell, "The Making of a Man," *Moody* (May 1992): 4.

4. H. Norman Wright, *What Men Want* (Ventura, Calif.: Regal 1996), 47–48.

5. Gordon Dalbey, *Fight Like a Man* (Wheaton, Ill.: Tyndale, 1995), 238.

6. Gordon Dalbey, *Healing the Masculine Soul*, 28.

Chapter 5: Men Are from Mars, Women Are from the Mall

1. Tim Allen, *Don't Stand Too Close to a Naked Man* (New York: Hyperion, 1994), 89.

2. John Gray, *Men, Women and Relationships* (New York: Harper, 1993), 2.

3. John Gray, *Men Are from Mars, Women Are from Venus* (New York: HarperCollins, 1992), 43.

Chapter 6: Feelings—Can You Trust Them?

1. Tom L. Eisenman, *Temptations Men Face* (Downers Grove, Ill.: InterVarsity, 1991), 38.

2. Gary J. Oliver, *Real Men Have Feelings Too* (Chicago: Moody, 1993), 37.

3. H. Norman Wright, *What Men Want* (Ventura, Calif.: Regal, 1996), 32.

4. Charles Swindoll, *Flying Closer to the Flame* (Dallas: Word, 1993), 156.

Chapter 8: Relationships (and Other Girl Stuff)

1. Dave Barry, *Complete Guide to Guys* (New York: Random House, 1995), 64.

2. Ibid., 59.

3. Carol Gilligan, *In a Different Voice* (Cambridge, Mass.: Harvard Univ., 1982), 8.

4. James S. Bell Jr. and Stan Campbell, *A Return to Virtue* (Chicago: Northfield, 1995), 70.

5. John Gray, *Men, Women and Relationships* (New York: Harper, 1993), 123–24.

6. John Gray, *Men Are from Mars, Women Are from Venus* (New York: HarperCollins, 1992), 140–41.

7. James Osterhaus, *Bonds of Iron* (Chicago: Moody, 1994), 25.

8. Ibid., 68.

Chapter 9: The Blame Game, Pride, and Other Unmanly Acts

1. Patrick M. Morley, *The Man in the Mirror* (Brentwood, Tenn.: Wolgemuth & Hyatt, 1989), 190.

Chapter 10: I Want to Be a Macho Man

1. H. Norman Wright, *What Men Want* (Ventura, Calif.: Regal, 1996), 44.

2. Ibid., 48.

3. As quoted by Gary J. Oliver in John Trent, gen. ed., *Go the Distance* (Colorado Springs: Focus on the Family, 1996), 27.

4. Adapted from Gary J. Oliver in Trent, *Go the Distance*, 27.

5. Adapted from Jim Burns and Greg McKinnon, *Illustrations, Stories and Quotes to Hang Your Message On* (Ventura, Calif.: Gospel Light, 1997), 119.

Chapter 11: Climbing the Ladder

1. Gary J. Oliver, "The Cult of Success," *New Man* (September 1997): 72

2. Patrick M. Morley, *The Seven Seasons of a Man's Life* (Nashville: Thomas Nelson, 1995), 151–52.

3. Oliver, "The Cult of Success," 74.

4. Stephen R. Covey, *The 7 Habits of Highly Effective People* (New York: Simon & Schuster, 1989), 19.

5. Adapted from Tim Smith, *8 Habits of an Effective Youth Worker* (Colorado Springs: Chariot Victor, 1995), 56.

6. Oswald Chambers, *My Utmost for His Highest* (Grand Rapids: Discovery House, 1992), August 4 Devotional.

Chapter 12: Do Brides Come with Scheduled Maintenance?

1. Gary Chapman, *The Five Love Languages* (Chicago: Northfield, 1995), 174.

2. Gary Kinnaman, *Learning to Love the One You Marry* (Ann Arbor, Mich.: Servant, 1997), 70–71.

3. Les Parrott III and Leslie Parrott, *Saving Your Marriage Before It Starts* (Grand Rapids: Zondervan, 1995), 16.

4. Gene A. Getz, *The Measure of a Man* (Ventura, Calif.: Regal, 1974), 33.

5. Ibid.

Chapter 13: The Relaxed Father

1. Mary Pipher, *Reviving Ophelia: Saving the Selves of Adolescent Girls* (New York: Ballantine, 1994), 116.

Chapter 15: Me? A Spiritual Leader?!

1. Gene A. Getz, *The Measure of a Man* (Ventura, Calif.: Regal, 1974), 15.

2. R. Kent Hughes, *Disciplines of a Godly Man* (Wheaton, Ill.: Crossway, 1991), 81.

3. H. Norman Wright, *What Men Want* (Ventura, Calif.: Regal, 1996), 162.

4. Jerry Bridges, *The Practice of Godliness* (Colorado Springs: NavPress, 1983), 91.